CREATIVE VISUALIZATION

"An open mind and heart plus the desire to greatly enrich one's life are all you need to bring to this book—then prepare yourself for some rather startling and truly marvelous results."

—*New Age Magazine*

"Inspiring and uplifting."

—*Bay Area Lifestyle*

"A clear and practical guide."
—Irving Oyle, M.D., author of
The New American Medicine Show

"Shakti Gawain provides us with the means to be our own instruments in dramatically and positively changing our lives."

—Kay Kaiser Cook,
Mothering

BANTAM NEW AGE BOOKS

This important imprint includes books in a variety of fields and disciplines and deals with the search for meaning, growth, and change. They are books that circumscribe our times and our future.

Ask your bookseller for the books you have missed.

BETWEEN HEALTH AND ILLNESS by Barbara B. Brown
THE CASE FOR REINCARNATION by Joe Fisher
THE COSMIC CODE by Heinz R. Pagels
CREATIVE VISUALIZATION by Shakti Gawain
THE DANCING WU LI MASTERS by Gary Zukav
ECOTOPIA by Ernest Callenbach
AN END TO INNOCENCE by Sheldon Kopp
ENTROPY by Jeremy Rifkin with Ted Howard
THE FIRST THREE MINUTES by Steven Weinberg
FOCUSING by Dr. Eugene T. Gendlin
GRIST FOR THE MILL by Ram Dass
THE HEART OF HEALING by Bruce Davis and
    Genny Wright Davis
THE HEART OF PHILOSOPHY by Jacob Needleman
I CHING: A NEW INTERPRETATION FOR MODERN
    TIMES by Sam Reifler
IF YOU MEET THE BUDDHA ON THE ROAD, KILL
    HIM! by Sheldon Kopp
IN SEARCH OF SCHRÖDINGER'S CAT
    by John Gribbin
INFINITY AND THE MIND by Rudy Rucker
KISS SLEEPING BEAUTY GOODBYE
    by Madonna Kolbenschlag

THE LIVES OF A CELL by Lewis Thomas
LIVING WITH NUCLEAR WEAPONS
   by Carnesale/Doty/Hoffman/Huntington/Nye and Sagan
MAGICAL CHILD by Joseph Chilton Pearce
THE MEDUSA AND THE SNAIL by Lewis Thomas
MIND AND NATURE by Gregory Bateson
THE MIND'S I by Douglas R. Hofstadter
   and Daniel C. Dennett
MISSILE ENVY by Dr. Helen Caldicott
NEW RULES by Daniel Yankelovich
ON HUMAN NATURE by Edward O. Wilson
THE ONE-STRAW REVOLUTION by Masanobu Fukuoka
ORDER OUT OF CHAOS by Ilya Prigogine and
   Isabelle Stengers
PROSPERING WOMAN by Ruth Ross
REENCHANTMENT OF THE WORLD by Morris Berman
SEVEN TOMORROWS by Hawken, Ogilvy, and Schwartz
SPACE-TIME AND BEYOND by Bob Toben and Alan Wolf
THE SPHINX AND THE RAINBOW by David Loye
STALKING THE WILD PENDULUM by Itzhak Bentov
STRESS AND THE ART OF BIOFEEDBACK
   by Barbara B. Brown
SUPERMIND by Barbara B. Brown
THE TAO OF PHYSICS, Revised Edition, by Fritjof Capra
TO HAVE OR TO BE? by Erich Fromm
THE TURNING POINT by Fritjof Capra
THE WAY OF THE SHAMAN: A Guide to Power and
   Healing by Michael Harner
ZEN AND THE ART OF MOTORCYCLE MAINTENANCE
   by Robert M. Pirsig
THE ZEN ENVIRONMENT by Marian Mountain

CREATIVE VISUALIZATION

Shakti Gawain

A BANTAM NEW AGE BOOK

BANTAM BOOKS
TORONTO · NEW YORK · LONDON · SYDNEY · AUCKLAND

This book is dedicated
to
you

This low-priced Bantam Book
has been completely reset in a type face
designed for easy reading, and was printed
from new plates. It contains the complete
text of the original hard-cover edition.
NOT ONE WORD HAS BEEN OMITTED.

CREATIVE VISUALIZATION

A Bantam Book / published by arrangement with
Whatever Publishing, Inc.

PRINTING HISTORY

Whatever Publishing edition published March 1979
7 printings through January 1982
Bantam edition / October 1982
7 printings through April 1985

New Age and the accompanying figure design
as well as the statement "a search for meaning,
growth and change" are trademarks of
Bantam Books, Inc.
Artwork by Rainbow Canyon

ISBN 0-553-24147-8

Published simultaneously in the United States and Canada

Bantam Books are published by Bantam Books, Inc. Its trademark,
consisting of the words "Bantam Books" and the portrayal of a
rooster, is Registered in U.S. Patent and Trademark Office and in
other countries. Marca Registrada. Bantam Books, Inc., 666 Fifth
Avenue, New York, New York 10103.

PRINTED IN THE UNITED STATES OF AMERICA

O   16   15   14   13   12   11   10   9   8

Acknowledgments

Thank you Mark Allen and Dean Campbell for your love and support in writing this book and in all other ways. Thank you Rainbow Canyon and Lorena Laforest Bass for your beautiful artwork and your beautiful friendship. And special thanks to my mother, Chi-uh, for all your love, wisdom, and encouragement.

I'd also like to thank all the incredible teachers who have contributed so much to my life and happiness, as well as to the understanding that has been channeled into this book. Some of you I have known as gurus, some as personal friends and lovers, and others of you have come to me in the form of books. To all of you I send my love and deep appreciation.

Last but not least I'd like to acknowledge and thank my own inner guide who keeps showing me the way . . . reminding me how beautiful life really is . . . and who actually is responsible for writing this book.

Contents

A Letter to my Readers   xi
Part One: Basics of Creative Visualization   1
  What is Creative Visualization?   2
  How Creative Visualization Works   5
  A Simple Exercise in Creative Visualization   9
  It's Important to Relax   11
  How to Visualize   13
  Four Basic Steps for Effective Creative
    Visualization   16
  Creative Visualization Works Only for Good   19
  Affirmation   21
  A Spiritual "Paradox"   27
Part Two: Using Creative Visualization   31
  Making Creative Visualization Part of Your Life 32
  Being, Doing, and Having   35
  Three Necessary Elements   37
  Contacting Your Higher Self   39
  Going With the Flow   42
  Prosperity Programming   45
  Accepting Your Good   49
  Outflowing   53
  Healing   57

Part Three: Meditations and Affirmations   63
  Grounding Yourself and Running Energy   64
  Opening the Energy Centers   66
  Creating Your Sanctuary   68
  Meeting Your Guide   70
  Pink Bubble Technique   73
  Healing Meditations   74
  Invocation   78
  Ways to Use Affirmations   80
Part Four: Special Techniques   85
  A Creative Visualization Notebook   86
  Clearing   89
  Writing Affirmations   96
  Setting Goals   98
  Ideal Scene   104
  Treasure Maps   106
  Health and Beauty   110
  Creative Visualization in Groups   114
  Creative Visualization in Relationships   116
Part Five: Living Creatively   119
  Creative Consciousness   120
  Discovering Our Higher Purpose   121
  Your Life Is Your Work of Art   123
Recommended Reading and Study   124

A Letter to my Readers

Dear Friends,

I decided to write this book because it seemed like the best way I could think of to share with others the many wonderful things I have learned which have so deepened and expanded my experience and enjoyment of life.

I do not consider myself by any means an expert on the art of creative visualization. I am a student of the subject, and the more I study and use creative visualization myself, the more I discover how vast and deep is its potential . . . truly it is as infinitely creative as your own imagination.

This book is meant as an introduction and workbook for learning and using creative visualization. Very little of the material is original to me; it is a synthesis of the most practical and useful ideas and techniques that I've learned in my personal study.

My sources are many. I've included at the end a list of books, tapes, records, and courses which have been most important to me, and which I think you will find interesting and helpful.

One note: this book contains many different techniques. You will probably find that it works best not to try to absorb them all at once, but more gradually. I suggest that you read the book slowly, trying some of the exercises as you go along, and giving yourself the chance to absorb them deeply. Or you might want to read it once through, then re-read more slowly.

Please feel free to write me with your comments and suggestions (c/o Whatever Publishing). Although I may not be able to reply personally to all your communications, I do very much value your feedback.

This book is my gift to you in love . . . may it be a blessing to you . . . may it help you to bring more and more joy, satisfaction, and beauty into your life . . . may it nurture the light that is shining within you . . .

Enjoy!

Love,
Shakti

Part One

Basics
of
Creative
Visualization

*Every moment of your life is infinitely creative
and the universe is endlessly bountiful.
Just put forth a clear enough request,
and everything your heart desires must come to you.*

What is Creative Visualization?

Creative visualization is the technique of using your imagination to create what you want in your life. There is nothing at all new, strange, or unusual about creative visualization. You are already using it every day, every minute in fact. It is your natural power of imagination, the basic creative energy of the universe which you use constantly, whether or not you are aware of it.

In the past, many of us have used our power of creative visualization in a relatively unconscious way. Because of our own deep-seated negative concepts about life, we have automatically and unconsciously expected and imagined lack, limitation, difficulties, and problems to be our lot in life. To one degree or another that is what we have created for ourselves.

This book is about learning to use your natural creative imagination in a more and more conscious way, as a technique to create what you *truly* want—love, fulfillment, enjoyment, satisfying relationships, rewarding work, self-expression, health, beauty, prosperity, inner peace and harmony . . . whatever your heart desires. The use of creative visualization gives us a key to tap into the natural goodness and bounty of life.

Imagination is the ability to create an idea or mental picture in your mind. In creative visualization you use your imagination to create a clear image of something you wish to manifest. Then you continue to focus on the idea or picture regularly, giving it positive energy until it becomes objective reality . . . in other words, until you actually achieve what you have been visualizing.

Your goal may be on any level—physical, emotional, mental, or spiritual. You might imagine yourself with a new home, or a new job, or having a beautiful relationship, or feeling calm and serene, or perhaps with an improved memory and learning ability. Or you might picture yourself handling a difficult situation effortlessly, or simply see yourself as a radiant being, filled with light and love. You can work on any level, and all will have results . . . through experience you will find the particular images and techniques which work best for you.

Let us say, for example, that you have difficulty getting along with someone and you would like to create a more harmonious relationship with that person.

After relaxing into a deep, quiet, meditative state of mind, you mentally imagine the two of you relating and communicating in an open, honest, and harmonious way. Try to get a feeling in yourself that your mental image is possible; experience it as if it is already happening.

Repeat this short, simple exercise often, perhaps two or three times a day or whenever you think about it. If you are sincere in your desire and intention, and truly open to change, you will soon find that the relationship is becoming easier and more flowing, and that the other person seems to become more agreeable and easier to communicate with. Eventually you will find that the problem will resolve itself completely, in one way or another, to the benefit of all parties concerned.

It should be noted here that this technique *cannot* be used to "control" the behavior of others or cause them to do something against their will. Its effect is to dissolve our internal barriers to natural harmony and self-realization, allowing everyone to manifest in their most positive aspect.

*   *   *

To use creative visualization it is not necessary to believe in any metaphysical or spiritual ideas, though you must be willing to entertain certain concepts as being possible. It is not necessary to "have faith" in any power outside yourself.

The only thing necessary is that you have the desire to enrich your knowledge and experience, and an open enough mind to try something new in a positive spirit.

Study the principles, try the techniques with an open mind and heart, and then judge for yourself whether they are useful to you.

If so, continue using and developing them, and soon the changes in yourself and your life will probably exceed anything you could have originally dreamed of . . .

Creative visualization is magic in the truest and highest meaning of the word. It involves understanding and aligning yourself with the natural principles that govern the workings of our universe, and learning to use these principles in the most conscious and creative way.

If you had never seen a gorgeous flower or a spectacular sunset before, and someone described one to you, you might consider it to be a miraculous thing (which it truly is!). Once you saw a few yourself, and began to learn something about the natural laws involved, you would begin to understand how they are formed and it would seem natural to you and not particularly mysterious.

The same is true of the process of creative visualization. What at first might seem amazing or impossible to the very limited type of education our rational minds have received, becomes perfectly understandable once we learn and practice with the underlying concepts involved.

Once you do so, it may seem that you are working miracles in your life . . . and you truly will be!

How Creative Visualization Works

In order to understand how creative visualization works, it's useful to look at several interrelated principles:

The physical universe is energy

The scientific world is beginning to discover what metaphysical and spiritual teachers have known for centuries. Our physical universe is not really composed of any "matter" at all; its basic component is a kind of force or essence which we can call *energy*.

Things appear to be solid and separate from one another on the level at which our physical senses normally perceive them. On finer levels, however, atomic and subatomic levels, seemingly solid matter is seen to be smaller and smaller particles within particles, which eventually turn out to be just pure energy.

Physically, we are all energy, and everything within and around us is made up of energy. We are all part of one great energy field. Things which we perceive to be solid and separate are in reality just various forms of our essential energy which is common to all. We are all one, even in a literal, physical sense.

The energy is vibrating at different rates of speed, and thus has different qualities, from finer to denser.

5

Thought is a relatively fine, light form of energy and therefore very quick and easy to change. Matter is relatively dense, compact energy, and therefore slower to move and change. Within matter there is great variation as well. Living flesh is relatively fine, changes quickly, and is easily affected by many things. A rock is a much denser form, slower to change and more difficult to affect. Yet even rock is eventually changed and affected by the fine, light energy of water, for example. All forms of energy are interrelated and can affect one another.

Energy is magnetic

One law of energy is this: energy of a certain quality or vibration tends to attract energy of a similar quality and vibration.

Thought and feelings have their own magnetic energy which attracts energy of a similar nature. We can see this principle at work, for instance, when we "accidentally" run into someone we've just been thinking of, or "happen" to pick up a book which contains exactly the perfect information we need at that moment.

Form follows idea

Thought is a quick, light, mobile form of energy. It manifests instantaneously, unlike the denser forms such as matter.

When we create something, we always create it first in a thought form. A thought or idea always precedes manifestation. "I think I'll make dinner" is the idea which precedes creation of a meal. "I want a new dress," precedes going and buying one; "I need a job" precedes finding one, and so on.

An artist first has an idea or inspiration, then creates a painting. A builder first has a design, then builds a house.

The idea is like a blueprint; it creates an image of the form, which then magnetizes and guides the physical energy to flow into that form and eventually manifests it on the physical plane.

The same principle holds true even if we do not take direct physical action to manifest our ideas. Simply having an idea or thought, holding it in your mind, is an energy which will tend to attract and create that form on the material plane. If you constantly think of illness, you eventually become ill; if you believe yourself to be beautiful, you become so.

The law of radiation and attraction

This is the principle that whatever you put out into the universe will be reflected back to you. "As you sow, so shall you reap."

What this means from a practical standpoint is that we always attract into our lives whatever we think about the most, believe in most strongly, expect on the deepest levels, and/or imagine most vividly.

When we are negative and fearful, insecure or anxious we will tend to attract the very experiences, situations, or people that we are seeking to avoid. If we are basically positive in attitude, expecting and envisioning pleasure, satisfaction and happiness, we will attract and create people, situations, and events which conform to our positive expectations. So the more positive energy we put into imaging what we want, the more it begins to manifest in our lives.

Using creative visualization

The process of change does not occur on superficial levels, through mere "positive thinking." It involves exploring, discovering, and changing our deepest, most basic attitudes toward life. That is why learning to use creative visualization can become a process of deep and meaningful growth. In the process we often discover ways in which we have been holding ourselves back, blocking ourselves from achieving satisfaction and fulfillment in life through our fears and negative concepts. Once seen clearly, these limiting attitudes can be dissolved through the creative visualization process, leaving space for us to find and live our natural state of happiness, fulfillment, and love . . .

* * *

At first you may practice creative visualization at specific times and for specific goals. As you get more in the habit of using it, and begin to trust the results it can bring you, you will find that it becomes an integral part of your thinking process. It becomes a continuous awareness, a state of consciousness in which you know that you are the constant creator of your life.

That is the ultimate point of creative visualization—to make every moment of our lives a moment of wondrous creation, in which we are just naturally choosing the best, the most beautiful, the most fulfilling lives we can imagine . . .

A Simple Exercise in Creative Visualization

Here is an exercise in the basic technique of creative visualization:

First, think of something you would like. For this exercise choose something simple, that you can *easily* imagine attaining. It might be an object you would like to have, an event which you would like to happen, a situation in which you'd like to find yourself, or some circumstance in your life which you'd like to improve.

Get in a comfortable position, either sitting or lying down, in a quiet place where you won't be disturbed. Relax your body completely. Starting from your toes and moving up to your scalp, think of relaxing each muscle in your body in turn, letting all tension flow out of your body. Breathe deeply and slowly, from your belly. Count down slowly from 10 to 1, feeling yourself getting more deeply relaxed with each count.

When you feel deeply relaxed, start to imagine the thing you want exactly as you would like it. If it is an object, imagine yourself with the object, using it, admiring it, enjoying it, showing it to friends. If it is a situation or event, imagine yourself there and everything happening just as you want it to. You may imagine what people are saying, or any details that make it more real to you.

You may take a relatively short time or quite a few minutes to imagine this—whatever feels best to you. Have fun with it. It should be a thoroughly enjoyable experience, like a child daydreaming about what he wants for his birthday.

Now keeping the idea or image still in your mind, mentally make some very positive, affirmative statements to yourself (aloud or silently, as you prefer) about it, such as

"Here I am spending a wonderful weekend in the mountains. What a beautiful vacation," or

"I now have a wonderful, happy relationship with _____. We are really learning to understand each other."

These positive statements, called affirmations, are a very important part of creative visualization, which we will discuss in more detail later.

Always end your visualization with a firm statement to yourself

> *"This, or something better,*
> *now manifests for me*
> *in totally satisfying and harmonious ways,*
> *for the highest good of all concerned."*

This leaves room for something different and even better than you had originally envisioned to happen, and serves as a reminder to you that this process only functions for the mutual benefit of all.

If doubts or contradictory thoughts arise, don't resist them or try to prevent them. This will tend to give them a power they don't otherwise have. Just let them flow through your consciousness, and return to your positive statements and images.

Do this process only as long as you find it enjoyable and interesting. It could be five minutes or half an hour. Repeat every day, or as often as you can.

As you see, the basic process is relatively simple. To use it really effectively, however, usually requires some understanding and refinement.

It's Important to Relax

It's important to relax deeply when you are first learning to use creative visualization. When your body and mind are deeply relaxed, your brain wave pattern actually changes and becomes slower. This deeper, slower level is commonly called alpha level (while your usual busy waking consciousness is called beta level), and much research is currently being done on its effects.

The alpha level has been found to be a very healthful state of consciousness, because of its relaxing effect on mind and body. And interestingly enough, it has been found to be far more effective than the more active beta level in creating real changes in the so-called objective world, through the use of visualization. What this means for our practical purposes is that if you learn to relax deeply and do creative visualization, you will be able to make far more effective changes in your life than you will by thinking, worrying, planning, and trying to manipulate things and people.

If you have any particular way that you are accustomed to relaxing deeply or entering a quiet, meditative state, by all means use that method. Otherwise you may wish to continue using the method I've described in the previous chapter—breathing slowly and deeply, relaxing each muscle in your body in turn, and counting down from 10 to 1 slowly. If you have any trouble physically relaxing, you might want to seek yoga or meditation instruction which will be helpful in this regard. Usually though, a little practice in relaxation will make perfect.

Of course, a side benefit of all of this is that you will find deep relaxation healthful and beneficial both mentally and physically.

It is especially good to do creative visualization at night just before sleeping, or in the morning just after awakening, because at those times the mind and body are often already deeply relaxed and receptive. You might like to do it while lying in bed, but if you tend to fall asleep, it's best to sit up on the edge of the bed or in a chair, in a comfortable position with your spine straight and balanced. Having your spine straight helps the energy to flow and makes it easier to get a deep alpha wave pattern.

A short period of meditation and creative visualization done at mid-day will relax and renew you, and cause your day to flow more smoothly.

How to Visualize

Many people wonder exactly what is meant by the term "visualize." Some worry because they don't actually "see" a mental picture or image when they close their eyes and try to visualize.

Don't get stuck on the term "visualize." *It is not at all necessary to mentally see an image.* Some people say they see very clear, sharp images when they close their eyes and imagine something. Others feel that they don't really "see" anything, they just sort of "think about" it or imagine that they are looking at it, or become aware of a feeling impression. That's perfectly fine. We all use our imaginations constantly, it's impossible not to, so whatever process you find yourself doing when you imagine, is fine.

If you still don't feel sure what it means to visualize, read through each of these exercises, then close your eyes and try it:

Close your eyes and relax deeply. Think of some familiar room such as your bedroom or living room. Remember some familiar details of it, such as the color of the carpet, the way the furniture is arranged, how bright or dark it is. Imagine yourself walking into the room and sitting or lying down on a comfortable chair, couch or bed.

Now recall some pleasant experience you have had in the last few days, especially one involving good physical sensa-

13

tions such as eating a delicious meal, receiving a massage, swimming in cool water, or making love. Remember the experience as vividly as possible, and enjoy the pleasurable sensations once again.

Now imagine that you are in some idyllic country setting, perhaps relaxing on soft green grass beside a cool river, or wandering through a beautiful, lush forest. It can be a place that you have been, or an ideal place where you would like to go. Think of the details, and create it any way that you would like it to be.

Whatever process you used to bring these scenes to your mind is your way of "visualizing."

There are actually two different modes involved in creative visualization. One is the receptive, the other is active. In the receptive mode we simply relax and allow images or impressions to come to us without choosing the details of them; we take what comes. In the active mode we consciously choose and create what we wish to see or imagine. Both these processes are an important part of creative visualization, and your receptive and active abilities will both be strengthened through practice.

Special Problems with Visualization

Occasionally a person has completely blocked his ability to visualize or imagine at will, and feels that he simply "can't do it." This type of block usually arises from a fear, and it can be worked through if the person desires to do so.

Usually a person blocks his ability to use creative visualization out of a fear of what he may encounter by looking inside himself—fear of his own unacknowledged feelings and emotions.

For example, a man in one of my classes was consistently unable to visualize, and kept falling asleep during the meditations. It turned out that he had once had a profoundly emotional experience during a visualization process, and he was afraid he would be embarrassed by becoming emotional in front of others.

The truth is that there is *nothing* within us that can hurt us; it is only our fear of experiencing our own feelings that can keep us trapped.

If anything unusual or unexpected arises during meditation, the best thing is simply to look at it fully, be with it and experience it as much as you can, and you will find that it loses any negative power over you. Our fears arise from things we don't confront. Once we are willing to look *fully* and *deeply* at the source of a fear, it loses its power.

Fortunately, such problems with visualization are rare. As a rule, creative visualization comes naturally, and the more you practice it, the easier it will become.*

*I recommend the Silva Mind Control course for those desiring special practice with visualization. See recommended reading list.

Four Basic Steps for Effective Creative Visualization

1. Set Your Goal
Decide on something you would like to have, work toward, realize, or create. It can be on any level—a job, a house, a relationship, a change in yourself, increased prosperity, a happier state of mind, improved health, beauty, or better physical condition, or whatever.

At first, choose goals that are fairly easy for you to believe in, that you feel are possible to realize in the fairly near future. That way you won't have to deal with too much negative resistance in yourself, and you can maximize your feelings of success as you are learning creative visualization. Later, when you have more practice, you can take on more difficult or challenging problems.

2. Create a Clear Idea or Picture
Create an idea or mental picture of the object or situation exactly as you want it. You should think of it in the present tense as *already* existing the way you want it to be. Picture yourself with the situation as you desire it, now. Include as many details as you can.

You may wish to make an actual physical picture of it as well, by making a treasure map (described in detail later). This is an optional step, not at all necessary, but often helpful (and fun!).

3. Focus on it Often

Bring your idea or mental picture to mind often, both in quiet meditation periods, and also casually throughout the day when you happen to think of it. In this way it becomes an integrated part of your life, it becomes more of a reality for you, and you project it more successfully.

Focus on it clearly, yet in a light, gentle way. It's important not to feel like you are striving too hard for it or putting an excessive amount of energy into it—that would tend to hinder rather than help.

4. Give it Positive Energy

As you focus on your goal, think about it in a positive, encouraging way. Make strong positive statements to yourself: that it exists, that it has come or is now coming to you. See yourself receiving or achieving it. These positive statements are called "affirmations." While you are using affirmations, try to temporarily suspend any doubts or disbelief you may have, at least for the moment, and practice getting the feeling that that which you desire is very real and possible.

Continue to work with this process until you achieve your goal, or no longer have the desire to do so. Remember that goals often change before they are realized, which is a perfectly natural part of the human process of change and growth. So don't try to prolong it any longer than you have energy for it—if you lose interest it may mean that it's time for a new look at what you want.

If you find that a goal has changed for you, be sure to acknowledge that to yourself. Get clear in your mind about the fact that you are no longer focusing on your previous goal. End cycle on the old, and begin cycle on the new. This helps you avoid getting confused, or feeling like you've "failed" when you have simply changed.

When you achieve a goal, be sure to acknowledge consciously to yourself that it has been completed.

Often we achieve things which we have been desiring and visualizing, and we forget to even notice that we have succeeded! So give yourself some appreciation and a pat on the back, and be sure to thank the universe for fulfilling your requests.

Creative Visualization Works Only for Good

Don't fear that the power of creative visualization can be used for harmful ends. Creative visualization is a means of unblocking or dissolving the barriers we ourselves have created to the naturally harmonious, abundant and loving flow of the universe. It is only truly effective when it is used in alignment with our highest goals and purposes, for the highest good of all beings.

If someone should attempt to use this powerful technique for a harmful or destructively selfish end, he would only be demonstrating his ignorance of the law of karma. This is the same basic principle as the law of radiation and attraction, "as you sow, so shall you reap." Whatever you try to create for another will always boomerang back to you. That includes both loving, helpful, or healing actions and negative, destructive ones. This means, of course, that the more you use creative visualization to love and serve others as well as your own highest ends, the more love, happiness, and success will just naturally find their way to you.

Just to make sure that you are aware of this, it's good to always add the following phrase to any creative visualization process you do:

"This, or something better,
now manifests for me

*in totally satisfying and harmonious ways
for the highest good of all concerned.''*

As an example, if you are visualizing getting a promotion on your job, don't picture the person above you being fired, but imagine him or her moving on to other, better things or a better, more fulfilling job, so that it works out for the good of all. You don't need to understand or figure out *how* that will happen, or try to decide what is the best way it could work out; simply assume that it is working out for the best, and let universal intelligence take care of the details.

Affirmation

Affirmations are one of the most important elements of creative visualization. To affirm means to "make firm." An affirmation is a strong, positive statement that something is *already* so. It is a way of "making firm" that which you are imaging.

Most of us are aware of the fact that we have a nearly continuous inner "dialogue" going on in our minds. The mind is busy "talking" to itself, keeping up an endless commentary about life, the world, our feelings, our problems, other people, etc.

The words and ideas that run through our minds are very important. Most of the time we aren't consciously aware of this stream of thoughts, and yet what we are "telling ourselves" in our minds is the basis on which we form our experience of reality. Our mental commentary influences and colors our feelings and perceptions about what's going on in our lives, and it is these thought forms that ultimately attract and create everything that happens to us.

Anyone who has practiced meditation knows how difficult it can be to quiet this inner "mind talk," in order to connect with our deeper, wiser intuitive mind. One traditional meditation practice is to simply observe the inner dialogue as objectively as possible.

This is a very valuable experience, as it allows you to become consciously aware of the types of thoughts you habitually think. Many of these thoughts are like tape recordings of old patterns we've had all our lives. They are old "programming" we picked up long ago, which is still influencing what's happening to us today.

The practice of doing affirmations allows us to begin replacing some of our stale, worn out, or negative mind chatter with more positive ideas and concepts. It is a powerful technique, one which can in a short time completely transform our attitudes and expectations about life, and thereby totally change what we create for ourselves.

Affirmations can be done silently, spoken aloud, written down, or even sung or chanted. Even ten minutes a day of doing effective affirmations can counterbalance years of old mental habits. Naturally, the more frequently you remember to be conscious of what you're "telling yourself," and choose positive, expansive words and concepts, the more positive a reality you will create.

An affirmation can be any positive statement. It can be very general or very specific. There are an infinite number of possible affirmations; here are a few just to give you some ideas:

Every day in every way I'm getting better, better, and better.
Everything is coming to me easily and effortlessly.
I am a radiant being, filled with light and love.
I am naturally enlightened.
My life is blossoming in total perfection.
I have everything I need to enjoy my here and now.
I am the master of my life.
Everything I need is already within me.
Perfect wisdom is in my heart.
I am whole and complete in myself.
I love and appreciate myself just as I am.
I accept all my feelings as part of myself.
I love to love and be loved.
The more I love myself, the more love I have to give others.
I now give and receive love freely.

*I am now attracting loving, satisfying, happy relationships
into my life.*

*My relationship with _____ is growing happier and
more fulfilling every day.*

I now have a perfect, satisfying, well paying job.

*I love doing my work, and I am richly rewarded, creatively
and financially.*

I am an open channel of creative energy.

I am dynamically self-expressive.

I always communicate clearly and effectively.

*I now have enough time, energy, wisdom and money to
accomplish all my desires.*

*I am always in the right place at the right time, successfully
engaged in the right activity.*

It's okay for me to have everything I want!

This is a rich universe and there's plenty for all of us.

Abundance is my natural state of being. I accept it now!

Infinite riches are now freely flowing into my life.

Every day I am growing more financially prosperous.

The more I have, the more I have to give.

The more I give, the more I receive, and the happier I feel.

It's okay for me to have fun and enjoy myself, and I do!

I am relaxed and centered. I have plenty of time for everything.

I am now enjoying everything I do!

I feel happy and blissful just being alive.

I am vibrantly healthy and radiantly beautiful!

*I am open to receiving all the blessings of this abundant
universe!*

*_____ (you fill in the blank) is coming
to me, easily and effortlessly.*

*I have a wonderful job with wonderful pay. I do a wonderful
service in a wonderful way.*

*The light of God within me is producing perfect results in
every phase of my life now.*

*The light within me is creating miracles in my life here and
now.*

*I give thanks for divine restoration in mind, body, financial
affairs, and in all my relationships now.*

All things are now working together for good in my life.

I am now attuned to the divine plan of my life.

*I now recognize, accept, and follow the divine plan of my life
    as it is revealed to me step by step.*
*I give thanks now for my life of health, wealth, happiness,
    and perfect self-expression.*

Here are some important things to remember
about affirmations:

1. Always phrase affirmations in the present tense,
not in the future. It's important to create it as if it
already exists. Don't say, "I will get a wonderful new
job," but rather "I now have a wonderful new job."
This is not lying to yourself; it is acknowledging the
fact that everything is created *first* on the mental plane,
before it can manifest in objective reality.

2. Always phrase affirmations in the most positive
way that you can. Affirm what you *do* want, not what
you *don't* want. Don't say "I no longer oversleep in the
morning" but rather "I now wake up on time and full
of energy every morning." This insures that you are
creating the most positive possible mental image.

At certain times you may find it helpful to phrase
affirmations negatively, especially when you are working on clearing out specific emotional blocks or bad
habits; i.e. "I don't need to get tense in order to get
things accomplished." If so, you should always *follow*
this type of affirmation with a positive one which
describes that which you desire to create, i.e. "I now
stay deeply relaxed and centered, and everything is
accomplished easily and effortlessly."

3. In general, the shorter and simpler the affirmation
the more effective. An affirmation should be a clear
statement that conveys a strong feeling; the more feeling it conveys, the stronger the impression it makes on
your mind. Affirmations that are long, wordy and the-
oretical lose their emotional impact and become a "head
trip."

4. Always choose affirmations that feel totally right
for you. What works for one person may not work at

all for another. An affirmation should feel positive, expansive, freeing, and/or supportive. If it doesn't, find another one, or try changing the words until it feels right.

Of course, you may feel emotional resistance to any affirmation when you first use it, especially one which is really powerful for you and is going to make a real change in your consciousness. That is simply the ego's initial resistance to change and growth.

5. Always remember when doing affirmations that you are creating something new and fresh. *You are not trying to redo or change what already exists.* To do so would be to resist what *is*, which creates conflict and struggle.

Take the attitude that you are accepting and handling whatever already exists in your life, and at the same time every moment is a new opportunity to begin creating exactly what you desire and will make you happiest.

6. Affirmations are not meant to *contradict* or *try to change* your feelings or emotions. It is important to accept and experience *all* your feelings, including so-called "negative" ones without attempting to change them. At the same time, affirmations can help you create a new point of view about life which will enable you to have more and more satisfying experiences from now on.

7. When using affirmations, try as much as possible to create a feeling of belief, an experience that they can be true. Temporarily (at least for a few minutes) suspend your doubts and hesitations, and put your full mental and emotional energy into them.

If doubts, resistance, or negative thoughts are getting in the way of doing your affirmations, do one of the clearing processes or the writing affirmations process given in section four of this book.

Rather than saying affirmations by rote, try to get the feeling that you really have the power to create that reality (which in fact you do!). This will make a big difference in how effective they are.

Affirmations can be used alone, or in combination with visualizing or imaging. You should always include affirmations as part of your regular creative visualization meditation periods. Later in the book I'll give you ideas for many other ways to use affirmations.

Affirmations are often most powerful and inspiring when they include references to spiritual sources. Mention of God, Christ, Buddha or any great master adds spiritual energy to your affirmation, and acknowledges the universal source of all things. You may prefer to use such phrases as divine love, the light within me, or universal intelligence.

Some examples:

Divine love is working through me here and now to create this.

The Christ within me is creating miracles in my life here and now.

I am one with my higher nature and I have infinite creative power.

My higher self is guiding me in everything that I do.

God lives within me and manifests in the world through me.

The light of God surrounds me, the love of God unfolds me, the power of God flows through me.
Wherever I am, God is, and all is well!

A Spiritual "Paradox"

Sometimes people who have studied eastern philosophy or are on a consciousness growth path feel a certain hesitation about using creative visualization when they first hear of it. Their conflict comes from the *apparent* paradox they see between the idea of "being here now," letting go of attachments and desires, and the idea of setting goals and creating what you want in life. I say *apparent* paradox, because in actuality there is no contradiction between the two teachings when they are understood on a deeper level. They are both important principles which must be understood and lived in order to become a conscious person. In order to explain how they fit together, allow me to share with you my viewpoint about the process of inner growth:

Most people in our culture have become cut off from their awareness of who they really are. They have temporarily lost their conscious connection with their higher selves and thus they have lost their own sense of power and responsibility for their lives. In some inner way, they have a sense of helplessness; they feel basically powerless to make real change in their lives or in the world. This inner feeling of powerlessness causes them to overcompensate by striving and struggling very hard to have *some* degree of power or control in their world.

Thus people become very goal oriented; they become

emotionally attached to things and people outside of themselves which they feel they need in order to be happier. They feel there is something "missing," inside themselves, and they become tense, anxious and stressed, continuously trying to fill up the gap, trying to manipulate the outside world in order to get what they want.

This is the state of being from which most people are setting goals and trying to create what they want in life, and unfortunately from this level of consciousness it doesn't work at all . . . either you set up so many obstacles to yourself that you *can't* succeed, or you *do* succeed in reaching your goals only to find that they don't bring you inner happiness.

It is at the point where we realize this dilemma that we begin to open up to a spiritual path. We realize that there simply has to be something more to life, and we begin to search for it.

We may go through many different experiences and processes on our search, but eventually we are gradually restored to ourselves. That is, we come back into an experience of our true selves, the God-like nature or the universal mind that is within us all. Through this experience we are eventually restored to our full spiritual power, the emptiness inside us is filled up *from within*, and we become radiant beings, sharing the light and love that comes from within us with everyone around us.

This is the process known as enlightenment, and I believe that it is an ongoing evolution for every individual, which cannot be complete until all our fellow beings are sharing in it. So we are all equally responsible for our own enlightenment and the enlightenment of all fellow beings on our planet . . .

Now to get back to our supposed paradox.

When you are coming out of the empty, grasping, manipulative condition, the first and foremost lesson to be learned is just to *let go*. You must relax, stop struggling, stop trying so hard, stop manipulating things and people to try to get what you want and need, in fact just stop *doing* so much and have an experience of just *being* for awhile.

When you do this, you suddenly discover that you're really perfectly okay, in fact you feel quite wonderful, just letting yourself be, and letting the world be, without trying to change things. This is the basic experience of *being here now* and it's what the Buddhist philosophy means by "letting go of attachment." It's a very freeing experience, and a most basic one on any path of self-awareness.

Once you have begun to have this experience more and more often, you are opening up the channel to your higher self, and sooner or later a great deal of natural creative energy will begin to flow through you. You start to see that you yourself are already creating your whole life and every experience that happens to you, and you become interested in creating more rewarding experiences for yourself and others. You begin to want to focus your energy toward the highest and most fulfilling goals that are real for you at any given moment. You realize that life is basically good, abundant, and fun, and that having what you want, without struggle and strain, is part of your natural birthright as a function of just being alive. This is the time when creative visualization can become a most important tool.

Here is a metaphor that I hope will make it even clearer:

Let us imagine that life is a river. Most people are clinging to the bank, afraid to let go and risk being carried along by the current of the river. At a certain point, each person must be willing to simply let go, and trust the river to carry him or her along safely. At this point he learns to "go with the flow" and it feels wonderful.

Once he has gotten used to being in the flow of the river, he can begin to look ahead and guide his own course onward, deciding where the course looks best, steering his way around boulders and snags, and choosing which of the many channels and branches of the river he prefers to follow, all the while still "going with the flow."

This analogy shows us how we can be enjoying our here and now, flowing with what is, and at the same time be guiding ourselves consciously toward our goals by taking responsibility for creating our own lives.

Remember, too, that creative visualization is a tool that can be used for any purpose, including one's own consciousness growth. It is often very helpful to use creative visualization in picturing yourself as a more relaxed, open person, flowing, living in the here and now, and always connected with your inner essence.

May you be blessed
with everything
your heart desires

Part Two

Using
Creative Visualization

Ask, and it shall be given you;
seek, and ye shall find;
knock, and it shall be opened unto you.

For every one that asketh, receiveth;
and he that seeketh, findeth;
and to him that knocketh it shall be opened.

Matthew 7:7,8

Making Creative Visualization Part of Your Life

As you can see from Part One, the basic technique of creative visualization is not difficult.

The important thing now is to learn to use it in a way that really works for you . . . that helps you to make positive change in your life. In order to use creative visualization most effectively it's helpful to understand certain concepts and learn some further techniques.

The most important thing to remember is to use creative visualization often, to make it a regular part of your life. Most people seem to find that it works best to practice it at least a little every day, especially when you are first learning.

I suggest that you have a regular creative visualization meditation period for fifteen minutes or so each morning when you wake up, and each evening before sleeping (these are the times when it is most effective), as well as the middle of the day if you can manage that. Always start your meditation periods with deep relaxation, then follow with any visualizations or affirmations you wish.

There are many different ways that creative visualization can be used, and it's up to you to remember to try them at appropriate times. Creative visualization may be a new way of thinking, a new way of living, and as such it will take some practice.

Try it out in different situations and different circumstances, and use it as often as you can for any type of problem solving. If you find yourself worrying or puzzling about anything, or feeling discouraged or frustrated about a problem, ask yourself whether there is a way you could use creative visualization to help you. Form a creative habit of using it at every appropriate moment.

Don't feel discouraged if you don't *immediately* feel totally successful with your creative visualization. Remember that most of us have years of negative thought patterns to overcome. It takes time to change some of these life-long habits. And many of us have some underlying feelings and attitudes which can slow us down in our efforts to live more consciously.

Fortunately creative visualization is such an innately powerful process that even five minutes of conscious, positive meditation can balance out hours, days, even years of negative patterns.

So be patient. It has taken a lifetime to create your world the way it is now. It may not necessarily change instantly (although it often does). With perseverance and a proper understanding of the process, you will succeed in creating what seem like many miracles in your life.

Two things I have found most important in my growth process with creative visualization are:

1. Regular reading of inspiring and uplifting books that help to keep me in touch with my highest ideals and aspirations. I usually keep a book by my bed and read a page or two each day. Many of my favorites are listed in the bibliography.

2. Having a friend or (ideally) a community of friends who are also tuned into learning to live more consciously and who will support you and help you in your efforts. Attending regular or occasional conscious-

ness classes or workshops can be an important way of getting this type of support, and giving it to others as well.

In the following chapters I will be giving you many different techniques, ideas, exercises, and meditations. Choose the ones that feel right to you and seem to work for you. There are many different levels and approaches to the creative visualization process, and I have tried to include a wide variety of possible practices. In any given situation, one may be appropriate and another may not. Follow the flow of your own energy, and use the ones that you feel drawn to.

For example, in a certain situation, you may try to do affirmations and find that you simply can't do it, or it doesn't feel like it's accomplishing anything. In that case you might want to try a clearing process, or get in touch with your higher self or spirit guide and ask what to do.

What works at one time may not at another; what works for one person may not for another. Always trust yourself and your own inner impulses.

If it feels like you are forcing, pushing, efforting, straining, don't do it.

If it feels positive, releasing, opening, strengthening, inspiring, do it.

Being, Doing, and Having

We can think of life as containing three levels, and we can call those levels beingness, doingness, and havingness.

Beingness is the basic experience of being alive and conscious. It is the experience we have in deep meditation, the experience of being totally complete and at rest within oneself.

Doingness is movement and activity, it stems from the natural creative energy that flows through every living thing and is the source of our vitality.

Havingness is the state of being in relationship with other people and things in the universe. It is the ability to allow and accept things and people into our lives; to comfortably occupy the same space with them.

Beingness, doingness and havingness are like a triangle where each side supports the others.

beingness

doingness havingness

They are not in conflict with each other.
They all exist simultaneously.

35

Often people attempt to live their lives backwards: They try to *have* more things, or more money, in order to *do* more of what they want, so that they will *be* happier.

The way it actually works is the reverse. You must first *be* who you really are, then *do* what you need to do, in order to *have* what you want.

The purpose of creative visualization is:
  To connect us with our beingness
  To help us focus and facilitate our doingness
  To increase and expand our havingness

Three Necessary Elements

There are three elements within you which determine how successfully creative visualization will work for you in any given situation:

1. *Desire.* You must have a true desire to have or create that which you have chosen to visualize. By desire I don't mean addictive, grasping desire, but a clear, strong feeling of purpose. Ask yourself "Do I truly, in my heart, desire this goal to be realized?"

2. *Belief.* The more you believe in your chosen goal and the possibility of attaining it, the more certain you will be to do so. Ask yourself "Do I believe that this goal can exist?" and "Do I believe that it is possible for me to realize or attain it?"

3. *Acceptance.* You must be willing to *accept* and *have* that which you are seeking. Sometimes we pursue goals without actually wanting to attain them; we are more comfortable with the process of pursuing. Ask yourself "Am I really willing to *have* this completely?"

The sum total of these three elements is what I call your *intention.* When you have total intention to create something—that is you deeply desire it, you completely believe that you can do it, and you are totally willing to have it—it simply cannot fail to manifest, and usually within a very short time.

The clearer and stronger your intention, the more quickly and easily your creative visualization will work. In any given situation, ask yourself about the condition of your intention. If it is weak or uncertain, it can often be strengthened by affirming:

I now have total intention to create this
here and now!

Contacting Your Higher Self

One of the most important steps in making your creative visualization work effectively and successfully is to have the experience of coming from "source."

Source means the supply of infinite love, wisdom, and energy in the universe. For you, source may mean God, or the universal mind, or the oneness of all, or your true essence. However we conceptualize it, it can be found here and now within each of us, in our inner being.

I like to think of contacting source as connecting with your higher self, the God-like being who dwells within you. Being in contact with your higher self is characterized by a deep sense of knowingness and certainty, of power, love, and wisdom. You know that you are creating your own world and that you have infinite power to create it perfectly.

We have all had experiences of being connected with our higher selves, although we may not have conceptualized it in that way. Feeling exceptionally high, clear, strong, "on top of the world," or "able to move mountains," are indications of being connected with your higher self; so is the experience of "falling in love" . . . when you feel wonderful about yourself and the world because your love for another human being is causing you to manifest as your highest self.

When you first become consciously aware of the

experience of your higher self, you will find that it seems to come and go rather sporadically. At one moment you may be feeling strong, clear and creative, the next moment you may be thrown back into confusion and insecurity. This seems to be a natural part of the process. Once you are aware of your higher self, you can call on it whenever you need it, and gradually you will find that it is with you more and more of the time.

The connection between your personality and your higher self is a two way channel, and it's important to develop the flow in both directions.

Receptive: When you quiet your personality during meditation, and come into a beingness space, you open the channel for higher wisdom and guidance to come to you through your intuitive mind. You can ask questions and wait for answers to come to you through words, mental images, or feeling impressions.

Active: When you are experiencing yourself as the creator of your universe, you make choices about what you desire to create, and channel the infinite energy, power, and wisdom of your higher self into manifesting your choices, through active visualization and affirmation.

When the channel is flowing freely in both directions, you are constantly being guided by your higher wisdom, and based on that guidance, you are making choices and creating your world in the highest, most beautiful way.

Almost any form of meditation will eventually take you to an experience of yourself as source, or your higher self. If you are not sure of what this experience is, don't worry about it. Just continue to practice relaxation, visualization, and affirmation. Eventually you will start experiencing certain moments during your meditation when there is a sort of "click" in your consciousness and you feel like things are really working; you may even experience a lot of energy flowing through you or a warm radiant glow in your body. These are signs that you are beginning to channel the energy of your higher self.

Here's an exercise in creative visualization that will help you tune into the feeling. You might wish to do this exercise regularly at the beginning of your meditation periods:

Sit or lie in a comfortable position. Relax completely . . . let all tension drain out of your body and mind . . . breathe deeply and slowly . . . relax more and more deeply.

Visualize a light within your heart—glowing radiant and warm. Feel it spreading and growing—shining out from you farther and farther until you are like a golden sun, radiating loving energy on everything and everyone around you.

Say to yourself silently and with conviction,

"Divine light and divine love are flowing through me and radiating from me to everything around me."

Repeat this over and over to yourself until you have a strong sense of your own spiritual energy. If you wish, use any other affirmations of your own power, light, creative ability, such as:

> *God is working through me now,*
> *or*
> *I am filled with divine light and creative energy*
> *or*
> *The light within me is creating miracles in my life here and now,*
> *or whatever phrase has meaning and power for you.*

Going With the Flow

The only effective way to use creative visualization is in the spirit of the way of the Tao—"going with the flow." That means that you don't have to "effort" to get where you want to go; you simply put it out clearly to the universe where you would like to go, and then patiently and harmoniously follow the flow of the river of life until it takes you there. The river of life sometimes takes a winding course toward your goal. It may even seem temporarily to be going in a different direction entirely, yet in the long run it is a more effortless and harmonious way to get there than through struggling and striving.

Going with the flow means holding onto your goals lightly (even though they may seem very important) and being willing to change them if something more appropriate and satisfying comes along. It is that balance between keeping your destination clearly in mind, and yet also enjoying all the beautiful scenes you encounter along the way, and even being willing to change your destination if life starts taking you in a different direction. In short, it means being firm, yet flexible.

If you have a lot of heavy emotions riding on whether you attain your goal (that is, if you will be upset if you don't get it) you will tend to work against yourself. In your fear of *not* getting what you want, you may actually be energizing the idea of not getting it as much or more than you are energizing the goal itself.

If you do find yourself very emotionally attached to a goal, it may be most effective and appropriate to work first on your feelings about the matter. You may have to take a good look at what you fear about *not* achieving the goal, and do affirmations to help you feel more confident and secure, or to help you face your fears.

For example:

> *The universe is unfolding perfectly*
> *I don't have to hang on*
> *I can relax and let go*
> *I can go with the flow*
> *I always have everything I need to enjoy my here and now*
> *I have all the love I need within my own heart*
> *I am a lovable and loving person*
> *I am whole in myself*
> *Divine love is guiding me and I am always taken care of*
> *The universe always provides*

You may find some of the clearing processes given later helpful. And once again I refer you to my recommended reading list for books that may offer help and insight.*

Of course it's perfectly okay to creatively visualize something to which you have a lot of attachment—and it will often work quite well. But if it doesn't, realize that your own inner conflict is sending out conflicting messages. In this case, it's important to relax and accept your feelings, accept the idea that you may not immediately realize your goal, and understand that resolving the conflict is probably an important area of growth for you and a wonderful opportunity to look more closely at your own attitudes about life.

If you get a feeling at any time while doing creative visualization that you are trying to *force* or *push* some-

---

*See especially *Handbook to Higher Consciousness* by Ken Keyes, Jr. and *Mystic Path to Cosmic Power* by Vernon Howard.

thing that doesn't want to happen, back off a little and ask your higher self whether this is really the best thing for you or whether you truly desire it. The universe may be trying to show you something better that you haven't even considered.

Prosperity Programming

A very important part of the whole creative visualization process is prosperity programming. This means having the understanding, or consciously taking the point of view, that the universe is totally abundant . . . it is a cornucopia of everything that your heart could ever desire, both on the material plane and on emotional, mental, and spiritual planes as well. Everything you need or want is here for the asking; you only need to *believe* that it is so, to truly *desire* it, and to be willing to *accept* it, in order to have whatever you wish.

One of the most common causes of failure to get what you want is "scarcity programming." This is an attitude or set of beliefs about life that goes something like this:

There isn't enough to go around . . .
Life is suffering . . .
It is immoral or selfish to have plenty when others don't have enough . . .
Life is hard, difficult, a vale of tears . . .
You must work hard and sacrifice for everything you gain . . .
It's more noble and spiritual to be poor . . .

and so forth.

These are all false beliefs. They are based on a lack of understanding of how the universe works, or a misunderstanding of some important spiritual principles. These beliefs are not of service to you or anyone else; they simply limit *all of us* from realizing our natural state of prosperity and plenty on all levels.

At the present time there is a reality in this world of starvation and poverty for many people, *but we do not need to keep creating and perpetuating that reality any longer.*

The fact is that there is more than enough to go around for every being on earth, if we are willing to open our minds to that possibility.* The universe *is* a place of great abundance and we are all naturally prosperous, both in material and spiritual wealth. Those who are not experiencing their world as rich and abundant, are on some level believing in scarcity programming rather than abundance. They have, through ignorance, bought into the popular belief in the inevitability of poverty and lack, and do not realize yet that the ultimate power of creation rests in the hands (or rather, minds) of each of us.

The truth about this earth is that it is an infinitely good, beautiful, nourishing place to be. The only "evil" comes from lack of understanding of this truth. Evil (ignorance) is like a shadow—it has no real substance of its own, it is simply a lack of light. You cannot cause a shadow to disappear by trying to fight it, stamp on it, by railing against it, or any other form of emotional or physical resistance. In order to cause a shadow to disappear, you must shine light on it.

Take a look at your belief system and see if you are holding yourself back by not believing sufficiently in the universal good. Can you actually realistically imagine yourself as a successful, satisfied, prosperous, fulfilled person? Can you really open your eyes to the goodness and beauty and abundance that are all around you? Can you imagine this world transformed into a

---

*I refer you to the Hunger Project source book, listed in the recommended reading.

happy, prosperous and enlightened environment in which everyone can flourish?

Unless you can create a context that the world is a good place to be that can potentially work for everyone, you will experience difficulty in creating what you want in your personal life.

This is because human nature is basically loving, and so most of us will not allow ourselves to have what we want as long as we believe that we might be depriving others in order to do so.

We have to understand in a deep way that having what we want in life contributes to the general state of human happiness and supports others in creating more happiness for themselves.

In a spirit of fun, try this exercise to stimulate your imagination and expand your ability to "have it all":

Cornucopia meditation
Relax completely in a comfortable position:

Picture yourself in any lovely natural environment—perhaps a green, open meadow with a lovely brook, or on white sand by the ocean. Take some time to imagine all the beautiful details, and see yourself fully enjoying and appreciating it. Now begin to walk, and soon find yourself in some totally different surrounding, perhaps a waving field of golden grain, or swimming in a lake. Continue to wander and explore, finding more and more exquisitely beautiful environments of great variety—mountains, forests, deserts, whatever suits your fantasy. Take a little time to appreciate each one . . .

Imagine yourself taking a boat to a lush tropical paradise, with incredible fruit on each tree. Picture yourself coming to a huge castle, where you are welcomed with an enormous feast, music, and dancing, then taken to the vast treasure room where you are presented with incredible jewels, precious metals, gorgeous clothes, more than you could ever use. Use your imagination, and see yourself wandering around the world, finding or being given everything you could ever want, in much greater quantity than you could even wish for.

Imagine the world as a magnificent paradise in which

everyone you meet is experiencing the same fullness and abundance that you are.

Enjoy it thoroughly. Go to other planets, if you wish, and find miraculous things there too. There are infinite possibilities! Eventually come home, happy and contented, and think about the fact that the Universe is truly a place of incredible wonder and abundance.

Affirmations:

This is a rich universe and there is plenty for all of us.
Abundance is my true state of being. I am now ready to accept it fully and joyously.
God is the unfailing, unlimited source of all my supply.
I deserve to be prosperous and happy, I am now prosperous and happy!
The more I prosper, the more I have to share with everyone else.
The universe is total abundance!
I'm ready now to accept all the joy and prosperity life has to offer me.
I now take responsibility for creating the world as a happy, abundant place for everyone.
Financial success is coming to me easily and effortlessly.
I am now enjoying great financial prosperity!
Life is meant to be fun and I'm now willing to enjoy it!
Infinite riches are now flowing freely into my life.
I am rich in consciousness and manifestation.
I now have more than enough money for my own personal use.
I now have a satisfying income of $———— per month.
Every day I'm growing more financially prosperous.
I am rich, well, and happy.

Accepting Your Good

In order to use creative visualization to create what you want in life, you must be willing and able to *accept* the best that life has to offer you—your "good."

Strange as it may seem, many of us have difficulty accepting the possibility of having what we want in life. This usually stems from some basic feelings of unworthiness which we took on at a very early age. The basic belief goes something like this: "I'm really not a very good (lovable, worthwhile) person so I don't deserve to have the best."

This belief is usually mixed with other, sometimes contradictory feelings that you really are perfectly good and deserving. But if you find that you have any difficulty imagining yourself in the most wonderful possible circumstances, or that you have thoughts like "I could never have that" or "That couldn't possibly happen to *me*," it might be well to take a good look at your self-image.

Your self-image is the way you see yourself, how you feel about yourself. It is often complex and multi-faceted. To get in touch with different aspects of your self-image, begin to ask yourself "How do I feel about myself right now?" at various times throughout the day, and in various different situations. Just begin to notice what kinds of ideas or images you hold in mind about yourself at different times.

One very interesting thing to do is to get in touch with your *physical* images of yourself by asking "How do I look to myself right now?" If you find yourself feeling awkward, ugly, fat, skinny, too big, too small, or whatever, it may be a clue to the fact that you aren't loving yourself enough to give yourself what you truly deserve—the best. It is often astounding to me to discover how many perfectly beautiful, attractive people frequently think of themselves as ugly, unworthy, undeserving.

Affirmations and creative visualization are a wonderful way of creating a more positive and loving self-image. Once you get in touch with the ways in which you are not loving yourself, begin to take every opportunity to tell yourself positive, appreciative, loving things. Notice when you are being mentally harsh or critical with yourself, and consciously begin being kinder and more appreciative. You will find this immediately helps you to be more loving towards others, as well.

Think of specific qualities that you do appreciate about yourself. In the same way that you can love a good friend while clearly seeing his or her faults and shortcomings, you can love yourself for all that you truly are, while still being aware that there are ways you need to grow and develop. It feels very good to do this for yourself, and it can really work wonders in your life.

Begin to tell yourself:

> *I am beautiful and lovable*
> *I am kind and loving, and I have a great deal to share with others*
> *I am talented, intelligent and creative*
> *I am growing more and more attractive every day*
> *I deserve the very best in life*
> *I have a lot to offer and everyone recognizes it*
> *I love the world and the world loves me*
> *I am willing to be happy and successful*

or whatever words seem appropriate and helpful to you.

It is often very effective to do this type of affirmation in the second person, using your own name:

"Susan, you are a brilliant and interesting person. I like you very much" or

"John, you are so warm and loving. People really appreciate that about you."

This way of talking directly to yourself is especially effective because much of our negative self-image comes from being convinced in various ways at an early age by other people that we are bad, stupid, or inadequate in some way.

Try to picture yourself as clearly as you can, and think of giving love to yourself, the same way you would to anyone else you care for. You might think of it as the parent in you giving love and appreciation to the child in you. Tell yourself:

"I love you. You are a very beautiful person. I appreciate your sensitivity and honesty."

Creative visualization is a great way to work on any physical problems you may feel you have. For example, if you feel you are too fat, you need to work on two things simultaneously:

1. Through affirmations and loving energy, start learning to love and appreciate yourself more *as you already are.*

2. Through creative visualization and affirmations, start creating yourself as you *want to be*—slim, trim, healthy, and happy. These techniques are extremely effective in making real changes.

These same two techniques hold true for working on any "problem" in the way you see yourself.

Remember, you are a new person at every new moment. Every day is a new day, and each one is an opportunity to realize the wonderful, loving, and lovable person you truly are . . .

In addition to improving your self-image, it is valuable to do affirmations about opening up to and accepting the goodness of the universe.

For example:

I am open to receiving the blessings of this abundant universe
Everything good is coming to me easily and effortlessly (any word you want can be substituted for 'everything good', i.e. love, prosperity, creativity, a perfect relationship)
I accept my good, which is flowing to me here and now
I deserve the best and the best is coming to me now
The more I receive the more I have to give

Here is a meditation you can do to improve your self-esteem and increase your capacity to handle the love and energy that the universe is ready and eager to flow in your direction:

Self-appreciation meditation
Imagine yourself in some everyday situation, and picture someone (maybe someone you know, or a stranger) looking at you with great love and admiration and telling you something they really like about you. Now picture a few more people coming up and agreeing that you are a very wonderful person. (If this embarrasses you, stick with it.) Imagine more and more people arriving and gazing at you with tremendous love and respect in their eyes. Picture yourself in a parade or on a stage, with throngs of cheering, applauding people, all loving and appreciating you. Hear their applause ringing in your ears. Stand up and take a bow, and thank them for their support and appreciation.

Some affirmations for self-appreciation:

I love and accept myself completely as I am.
I don't have to try to please anyone else. I like myself and that's what counts.
I am highly pleasing to myself in the presence of other people.
I express myself freely, fully and easily.
I am a powerful, loving, and creative being.

Outflowing

Another key principle is that of giving, or "outflowing." The universe is made up of pure energy, the nature of which is to move and flow. The nature of life is constant change, constant flux. When we understand this, we tune into its rhythm and we are able to give and receive freely, knowing that we never really lose anything, but constantly gain.

Once we begin to learn to *accept* the goodness of the universe, we naturally want to *share* it as well, realizing that as we give out of our energy, we make space for more to flow into us.

When, through insecurity (fear) and a feeling that there "isn't enough," we try to hold onto or cling to what we have, we begin to cut off this wonderful flow of energy. In hanging onto what we have, we fail to keep the energy moving and we don't make space for new energy to come to us.

Energy takes many forms, such as love, affection, appreciation and recognition, material possessions, money, friendship, etc. and the principles apply equally to all these forms.

If you look around you at those who are most unhappy, you'll find they are often people who have a "starved" feeling in some way, and are therefore in a very grasping posture toward life. They feel that life in general and other people in particular are not giving them what they need. It is as if they have a stranglehold on life, trying desperately to wring out the love and satisfaction they crave, yet actually choking off the supply. And many of us have a little of this tendency.

When we find that place within ourselves that is giving, we begin to reverse the flow. Giving happens not from a space of sacrifice, or self-righteousness, or an idea of spirituality, but for the pure *pleasure* of it—because it's fun. It can only come from a full, loving space.

We each have an infinite supply of love and happiness within us. We have been accustomed to thinking that we have to get something from outside us in order to be happy, but in truth it works the other way: we must learn to contact our inner source of happiness and satisfaction and flow it outward to share with others—not because it is virtuous to do so, but because it feels really good! Once we tune into it we just naturally want to share it because that is the essential nature of love, and we are all loving beings.

As we outflow our loving energy, we make room for more to flow into us. We soon discover that this process feels so good in itself we just want to do it more and more. And the more you share of yourself from this space, the more you seem to get from the world, because of the outflow-inflow principle. (Nature abhors a vacuum, so as you outflow you create space into which something must inflow.) Giving becomes its own reward.

When we fully understand and live this we have manifested our innately loving nature.

So you will find in your use of creative visualization, that the more basically "giving" orientation you have to life, the easier it will be to fulfill your dreams . . . but remember always that you can't continue to give unless you are equally open to receiving . . . and that "giving" also means giving to yourself . . .

When it comes to outflowing, practice makes perfect. You must consciously practice it in order to get the experience of how good it feels. Here are some exercises in outflowing you can try if you need some expansion in this area:

1. *Make a point to express more appreciation to others in as many ways as you can think of. Sit down right now and make a list of people to whom you would like to outflow love and appreciation, and think of a way you can do so to each one within the next week. Outflow can take the form of words, touching, a gift, a phone call or letter, money, or any sharing of your talents that makes another person feel good. Choose something that makes you feel especially good too, even if it's a little more difficult for you.*

Practice speaking more words of thanks, appreciation and admiration to people when you feel like it. "It was kind of you to help me." "I want you to know that I appreciate that." "Your eyes were shining and beautiful as you said that, and it made me feel good to see you." (We don't need to feel embarrassed!)

2. *Go through your things and find things you don't really want or use very often and give them to others who will appreciate them more.*

3. *If you're a person who tries to spend as little money as possible and always hunts for a bargain, try spending a little money each day unnecessarily. Buy the product that costs a few cents more instead of less, treat yourself to a little something extra, pay for a friend's coffee, donate to a good cause, etc. Even a small action of this sort is a visible demonstration to yourself that you have faith in the abundance that you have been affirming. Actions speak as loud as words in this case.*

4. *Tithe your income. Tithing is the practice of giving a percentage of your income to a church, spiritual organization, or any group that you feel is making a worthwhile contribution in the world. It is a way of supporting that energy, and at the same time acknowledging that all you receive comes from the universe (or God) and therefore you give a token back to the universal source. It doesn't matter what the*

percentage is—even tithing just one percent of your income will give you a continuous experience of outflowing. Just be sure to do it regularly.

5. Be creative. Think of other ways to outflow your energy into the universe for the good of yourself and others.

Healing

Healing Ourselves
Creative visualization is one of the most important tools we have for creating and maintaining good health.

One of the basic principles of holistic health is that we cannot separate our physical health from our emotional, mental, and spiritual states of being. All levels are interconnected and a state of "dis-ease" in the body is always a reflection of conflict, tension, anxiety, or disharmony on other levels of being as well. So when we have a physical disorder, it is inevitably a message for us to look deeply into our emotional and intuitive feelings, our thoughts and attitudes, to see what we can do to restore natural harmony and balance to our being. We must tune in and "listen" to the inner process.

There is constant communication between mind and body. The body perceives the physical universe, and sends messages to the mind about it; the mind interprets the perceptions according to its own individual past experience and its belief system, and signals the body to react in a way which it feels is appropriate. *If the mind's belief system (on a conscious or unconscious level) says that it is appropriate or inevitable to get sick in a certain situation, it will signal the body accordingly, and the body will obligingly manifest symptoms of illness;* it will in fact become ill. So the whole process is closely tied in with our deepest concepts and ideas about ourselves, life, and the nature of disease and health.

Creative visualization refers to the way in which we communicate from our mind to our body. It is the process of forming images and thoughts in our mind, consciously or unconsciously, and then transmitting them to the body as signals or commands.

Conscious creative visualization is the process of creating positive thoughts and images to communicate with our bodies, in place of negative, constrictive, literally "sickening" ones.

People get sick because they believe on an inner level that illness is an appropriate or inevitable response to some situation or circumstance, because it in some way seems to solve a problem for them or get them something that they need, or as a desperate solution to some unresolved and unbearable inner conflict.

Some examples of this are: the person who becomes ill because he has been "exposed" to a communicable disease (he believes it is inevitable or highly likely), the person who dies of the same disease as a parent or other member of her family (she has unconsciously programmed herself to follow the same pattern), the person who gets sick or has an accident in order to get out of work (either there's something he can't confront at work, or he won't allow himself the relaxation and quiet he needs unless he is sick), the person who gets sick in order to get love and attention (this was how she was able to get her parents' love as a child), the person who represses his feelings all his life and eventually dies of cancer (he cannot resolve the conflict between the pressure of his stored-up emotions, and his belief that it's not okay for him to express himself . . . so he eventually kills himself as a solution).

I do not mean to imply by these examples that I believe all illness is a simple problem with a pat explanation. As with all our problems, there are often many complex factors. I do intend to illustrate the fact that illness is a result of our mental concepts and beliefs, and that illness is an attempt to find a solution to a problem we are having inside ourselves. If we are willing to recognize and change our innermost beliefs, we can find more constructive solutions to our problems, and we can eliminate illness and disease altogether.

The most positive, powerful, healthy and healing consciousness can be created by taking this point of view:

We are all in essence perfect, spiritual beings. We are each a perfect expression of the universal mind or God consciousness that is within us.

As such, our natural birthright is radiant health, beauty, boundless energy, youthful vitality and joy throughout our lives.

There is in actual fact no evil or limitation. There is only ignorance or misunderstanding of the universal nature of good (or God), combined with our infinite creative abilities.

The only limitations on our health, beauty, energy, vitality, and joy come from our own self-created blocks, our own resistance to the goodness of life, based on fear and ignorance.

Our bodies are simply a physical expression of our consciousness. The concepts we hold of ourselves determine our health and beauty or the lack thereof. When we deeply change our concepts, our physical self follows suit. The body is continuously changing, replenishing, and rebuilding itself at every moment and it has no other pattern to follow in doing so except the guidance to it by the mind.

The more we bring our consciousness into alignment with our highest spiritual realization, the more our bodies will express our own individual perfection.

The natural outgrowth of this point of view is a more constructive attitude about illness. Rather than thinking of illness as an inevitable disaster or unavoidable misfortune, we think of it as a powerful and useful message. If we are suffering physically in some way, it is a message that there is something to be looked at within our consciousness, something to be recognized, acknowledged, and changed.

Often the message of illness is to be quieter and spend some time just being in contact with our inner self. Illness often forces us to relax, let go of all our busyness and "efforting," and drop into a deep, quiet level of consciousness where we can receive the nourishing energy that we need.

The healing always comes from within. When we allow ourselves quiet and inner contact regularly, we no longer need to get sick in order for our inner self to get our attention.

Illness and "accidents" are messages that our concepts need changing or some inner problem needs to be resolved. Get as quiet as you can, listen for your inner voice, and ask what the message is, or what it is that you need to understand in this situation. You may be able to accomplish this alone, or in some cases you may need a counselor, therapist, friend, or healer to assist and support you.

Creative visualization is the perfect tool for healing because it goes straight to the source of the problem—your own mental concepts and images. Begin to picture yourself and affirm to yourself that you are in perfect radiant health; see your problem as completely healed and cured. There are many different approaches that can be taken on many different levels; you need to find the particular type of affirmations and images that work best for you. I've given some suggestions in section three of this book, and you can find others in the recommended reading.*

Of course "preventative medicine" is always the best . . . If you have no health problems, so much the better; simply affirm and visualize that you will always remain healthy and vital; that way you will never have to worry about healing yourself. If you already have health problems, it will be comforting to know that

* I particularly recommend the books and tapes of Joel Goldsmith and *The Nature of Personal Reality* by Jane Roberts. Also the books of Catherine Ponder, the Marc Reymont tapes, and the Silva Mind Control course.

many "miraculous" cures are being accomplished every day, even for very serious illnesses, such as cancer, arthritis, heart disease, through the simple use of various forms of creative visualization.

In many cases, creative visualization is a completely effective therapy in itself. In other cases, because of the person's own belief system (i.e. it is difficult to let go of the concept that we need something outside ourselves to be healed), it is necessary to use other forms of treatment as well. *As long as you have an inner confidence in some form of therapy then by all means use it!* It will work if you desire and believe it will. But whatever type of treatment is used, from conventional medicine or surgery, to more holistic therapies such as acupuncture, yoga, massage, diet, and so on, *creative visualization is always a helpful supplement*, one that you can use in conjunction with anything else. Conscious use of creative visualization will speed and smooth the normal healing process amazingly.

Healing Others

The same principles that work in healing ourselves also work to heal others. The healing consciousness I outlined earlier is just as powerful in healing others as in healing oneself (sometimes even more so).

This is so because of the oneness nature of the universal mind. There is a part of our consciousness that is directly linked with that part in everyone else's consciousness. Since that part is also our link with divine omnipotence and omniscience, we *all* have incredible healing powers which we can tap into at will.

Just as the concepts we hold about ourselves determine our health or lack of health, the concepts we hold about others can support their health or lack of health. If a friend has a concept which has caused her to become ill, and we buy into or believe that concept of her illness, we are supporting her ill health, no matter how lovingly we may desire her to become well. On the other hand, if we hold the concept of her health and perfection strongly in mind, we will truly support her healing process. It is not even necessary for her to know anything about what we are doing; in fact it is sometimes better that she not consciously know.

It is an amazing thing, but simply changing your own concepts about another person and consciously holding and projecting an image of health and well-being can *instantly cure* someone in many cases, and speed and smooth their healing in many other cases.

I was brought up with a very scientific and rational background and education, and the ability to heal other people at a distance has been one of the hardest things for me to understand and accept. Yet I have seen it and experienced it too often to doubt it any longer.

I've found that in my experience the best way to work on healing is to picture myself as a clear channel for healing energy, the spiritual energy of the universe, to flow *through* me and to the person who needs it. I think of my higher self sending energy to the other person's higher self to support them in whatever they need to do to heal themselves. At the same time I picture them as they truly are . . . a divine being, a beautiful and perfect expression of God . . . naturally healthy and happy.

In section three I describe the healing methods that I have found work best for me. I encourage you to try them, and to discover your own.

Part Three

Meditations and Affirmations

*Thou shalt decree a thing,
and it shall be established unto thee:
and the light shall shine upon thy ways.*

Job 22:28

Grounding Yourself and Running Energy

This is a very simple visualization technique, and one which is good to do at the beginning of any meditation. The purpose of it is to get your energy flowing, dissolve any blocks, and keep you firmly connected to the physical plane so that you don't "space out" during meditation.

Sit comfortably with your back straight, either in a chair or cross legged on the floor. Close your eyes, breathe slowly and deeply, counting down from 10 to 1 until you feel deeply relaxed.

Imagine that there is a long cord attached to the base of your spine and extending down through the floor and way down into the earth. If you wish, you can imagine that this is like the root of a tree, growing deep into the ground. This is called a "grounding cord."

Now imagine that the energy of the earth is flowing up through this cord (and up through the soles of your feet if you are sitting in a chair) and flowing up through all parts of your body, and out through the top of your head. Picture this until you really feel the flow well established. Now imagine that the energy of the cosmos is flowing in through the top of your head, through your body and down through your grounding cord and your feet into the earth. Feel both these flows going in different directions, and mixing harmoniously in your body.

This meditation keeps you balanced between the cosmic energy of vision, fantasy, and imagination, and the stable, earthy energy of the physical plane . . . a balance which will increase your sense of well being and your power of manifestation.

Opening the Energy Centers

This is a meditation for healing and purifying your body, and for getting your energy flowing. It is an excellent one to do in the morning when you first wake up, or at the beginning of any meditation period, or anytime you want to be relaxed and refreshed:

Lie down on your back with arms at your sides or with hands clasped on your stomach. Close your eyes, relax and breathe gently, deeply and slowly.

Imagine that there is a glowing sphere of golden light surrounding the top of your head. Breathe deeply and slowly in and out five times while you keep your attention on the sphere of light, feeling it radiate from the top of your head.

Now allow your attention to move down to your throat. Again imagine a golden sphere of light emanating from your throat area. Breathe slowly in and out five times with your attention on this light.

Allow your attention to move down to the center of your chest. Once again imagine the golden light, radiating from the center of your chest. Again take five deep breaths, as you feel the energy expanding more and more.

Next put your attention on your solar plexus; visualize the sphere of golden light all around your midsection. Breathe into it slowly, five times.

Now visualize the light glowing in and around your pelvic area. Again take five deep breaths, feeling the light energy radiating and expanding.

Finally, visualize the glowing sphere of light around your feet, and breathe into it five more times.

Now imagine all six of the spheres of light glowing at once so that your body is like a strand of jewels, radiating energy.

Breathe deeply, and as you exhale, imagine energy flowing down along the outside of the left side of your body from the top of your head to your feet. As you inhale, imagine it flowing up along the right side of your body to the top of your head. Circulate it around your body this way three times.

Then visualize the flow of energy going from the top of your head down along the front of your body to your feet as you slowly exhale. As you inhale, feel it flow up along the back of your body to the top of your head. Circulate the flow in this direction three times.

Now imagine that the energy is gathering at your feet, and let it flow slowly up through the center of your body from your feet to your head, radiating from the top of your head like a fountain of light, then flowing back down the outside of your body to your feet. Repeat this several times, or as long as you wish.

When you finish this meditation you will be deeply relaxed, yet energized and exhilarated.

Creating Your Sanctuary

One of the first things you should do when you start using creative visualization is to create a sanctuary within yourself where you can go anytime you want to. Your sanctuary is your ideal place of relaxation, tranquillity and safety and you can create it exactly as you want it.

Close your eyes and relax in a comfortable position. Imagine yourself in some beautiful natural environment. It can be any place that appeals to you . . . in a meadow, on a mountaintop, in the forest, beside the sea. It could even be under the ocean, or on another planet. Wherever it is, it should feel comfortable, pleasant and peaceful to you. Explore your environment, noticing the visual details, the sounds and smells, any particular feelings or impressions you get about it.

Now do anything you would like to do to make the place more homelike and comfortable an environment for you. You might want to build some type of house or shelter there, or perhaps just surround the whole area with a golden light of protection and safety, create and arrange things there for your convenience and enjoyment, or do a ritual to establish it as your special place.

From now on this is your own personal inner sanctuary, to which you can return at any time just by closing your eyes and desiring to be there. You will always find it healing and relaxing to be there. It is also a place of special power for you, and you may wish to go there every time you do creative visualization.

You may find that your sanctuary spontaneously changes from time to time, or that you want to make changes and additions to it. You can be very creative in your sanctuary and have a lot of fun there . . . just remember to retain the primary qualities of peacefulness, tranquillity and a feeling of absolute safety.

Meeting Your Guide

Each one of us has all the wisdom and knowledge we ever need right within us. It is available to us through our intuitive mind, which is our connection with universal intelligence. However, we often find it difficult to connect with our higher wisdom. One of the best ways to do so is by meeting and getting to know our inner guide.

The inner guide is known by many different names, such as your counselor, spirit guide, imaginary friend, or master. It is a higher part of yourself, which can come to you in many different forms, but usually comes in the form of a person or being whom you can talk to and relate to as a wise and loving friend.

Here is an exercise to help you meet your spirit guide. If you wish, you can have a friend read this to you while you do the meditation. Otherwise, read through it first, close your eyes and do it.

Close your eyes and relax deeply. Go to your inner sanctuary and spend a few minutes there, relaxing, getting oriented. Now imagine that within your sanctuary you are standing on a path which stretches off into the distance. You start to walk up the path, and as you do so, you see in the distance a form coming toward you, radiating a clear, bright light.

As you approach each other you begin to see whether the form is a man or woman, how they look, how old they are, and how they are dressed. The closer they get, the more details you can see of their face and appearance.

Greet this being, and ask him or her what their name is. Take whatever name comes to you first, and don't worry about it.

Now show your guide around your sanctuary and explore it together. Your guide may point out some things that you've never seen there before, or you may enjoy just being in each other's presence.

Ask your guide if there is anything he or she would like to say to you, or any advice to give you at the moment. If you wish, you can ask some specific questions. You may get immediate answers, but if not, don't be discouraged, the answers will come to you in some form later.

When the experience of being together feels complete for now, thank your guide and express your appreciation, and ask him or her to come to meet you in your sanctuary again.

Open your eyes and return to the outside world.

People have many different types of experience in meeting their guides, so it is difficult to generalize. Basically if you feel good about your experience, then it's fine. It not, be creative and do whatever you need to do to change it.

Don't worry if you did not perceive your guide clearly and precisely. Sometimes they remain in the form of a glow of light, or a blurry, indistinct figure. The important thing is that you sense their power, their presence, and their love.

If your guide should come to you in the form of someone you know, that is fine, *unless* you don't feel particularly good about it. In that case, repeat the exercise and request that your guide come to you in a form that is easy and pleasant for you to relate to.

Don't be surprised if your guide seems eccentric or unusual in some way . . . the form in which they show themselves to us springs from our own creative mind which is limitless. For example, your guide may have a very unusual and surprising sense of humor, or an exotic name and a flair for the dramatic. Sometimes they don't communicate in words at all, but in a direct transmission of feeling impressions or intuitive knowledge.

Also your guide *may* change form and even name from time to time. Or you may have the same one for years. You may have more than one guide at the same time.

Your guide is there for you to call on anytime you need or want extra guidance, wisdom, knowledge, support, creative inspiration, love or companionship. Many people who have established a relationship with their guide meet them every day in their meditation.

Pink Bubble Technique

This meditation is simple and wonderfully effective.

Exercise:

Sit or lie down comfortably, close your eyes and breathe deeply, slowly, and naturally. Gradually relax deeper and deeper.

Imagine something that you would like to manifest. Imagine that it has already happened. Picture it as clearly as possible in your mind.

Now in your mind's eye surround your fantasy with a pink bubble; put your goal inside the bubble. Pink is the color associated with the heart, and if this color vibration surrounds whatever you visualize, it will bring to you only that which is in perfect affinity with your being.

The third step is to let go of the bubble and imagine it floating off into the universe, still containing your vision. This symbolizes that you are emotionally "letting go" of it. Now it is free to float around in the universe, attracting and gathering energy for its manifestation.

There is nothing more you need to do.

Healing Meditations

Healing Ourselves

Sit or lie down, breathe, and relax deeply. Starting with your toes, feet, legs, pelvis and so on, put your attention on each part of your body in turn and tell it to relax and let go of any tension. Feel all tension dissolving and draining away.

If you wish to, do the meditation on opening the energy centers in order to get your energy really flowing.

Now imagine golden, healing light energy all around your body . . . feel it . . . sense it . . . enjoy it.

If there is a particular part of your body that has been ill or in pain, ask that part of you whether it has a message for you. Ask whether there is something you need to understand or to do, right at this moment or in your life in general.

If you get an answer, do your best to understand and follow it. If you don't get an answer, just continue with the process.

Now send special loving, healing energy to that part of you, and any part of you that needs it, and see or feel it being healed. You may want to have your guide, or any master or healer, there to help you do the healing.

Picture the problem dissolving and flowing energy away, or whatever image works for you.

Now imagine yourself in perfect, radiant, natural good health. Think of yourself in different situations feeling good, active and healthy. See yourself as divinely, radiantly beautiful.

Affirmations:

*I have now transcended all patterns of illness. I'm free and
   healthy!*
I am now full of radiant health and energy.
I love and accept my body completely.
I am good to my body, and my body is good to me.
I am energetic and full of vitality.
My body is balanced, in perfect harmony with the universe.
I give thanks for ever increasing health, beauty, and vitality.
*I am a radiant expression of God. My mind and body now
   manifest divine perfection.*

From now on, each time you do this meditation,
picture yourself only in perfect health, with golden
healing light around you. Do not give any more power
or energy to the "problem" unless you feel that there's
something more that you need to understand about it.

Healing Others
This meditation is to be done alone, *not* in the other
person's presence. You may or may not wish to tell
them that you are doing healing meditations for them,
depending on how well they would accept that idea on
a personality level.

*Relax deeply and do whatever type of preparation you wish
in order to enter a deep, quiet state of mind.*

*Think of yourself as a clear channel through which the
healing energy of the universe is pouring. This energy does
not come from you personally, it comes from a higher source,
and you serve to focus and direct it.*

*Now picture or think of the person as clearly as you can.
Ask him if there is anything in particular he would like you
to do for him in your meditation. If so, do it to the best of
your ability, if it feels right to you.*

*If you feel the impulse to work on healing a particular part
of his body, or a particular problem, do so. Just see all
problems dissolved, everything being healed and functioning
perfectly.*

Then picture him surrounded in golden, healing light . . .

looking radiantly healthy and happy. Speak to him directly (in your mind); remind him that he is actually a perfect, god-like being and that no illness or affliction need have any power over him. Tell him that you support him in being totally healthy and happy, and that you will continue to send him your loving support and energy.

When you feel complete, open your eyes and come back to the outer world feeling refreshed, renewed, healthy and invigorated.

From now on, in your meditations see the person as perfectly well. Don't give any more mental energy or power to the illness; just keep seeing him as completely healed.

Healing In Groups

Healings are very powerful when done in groups.

If the person to be healed is present in the room, have him lie down in the center or sit in a chair (whichever is most comfortable) with everyone else seated in a circle around him.

Everyone should close their eyes, be quiet, and relax deeply, then begin to imagine sending healing energy to the person in the center. Remember that it is the healing energy of the universe which is being channeled through you. See the person surrounded in golden light, feeling well, and in perfect health.

If you wish, you can have everyone raise their hands with the palms facing out toward the person in the center, and feel the energy flowing out to him through your hands.

It is especially powerful to have everyone chant "OM" together for a few minutes while doing the healing, thus adding the healing vibration of sound to the process (to chant "OM" you sing a long, deep resonant note with the syllable a-a-au-m-m, holding it as long as you can, and repeating it over and over).

If the person is not present in the room, just inform everyone of his name and the city where he is, and then proceed as if he were there. The power of healing energy is not affected at all by distance, and

I have seen as many miraculous cures accomplished for people in distant cities as for those present in the room.

Healing meditation for pain

Here is a meditation technique you can do with a person who is experiencing a headache or any other specific pain:

Have the person lie down, close his eyes, and relax deeply. Have him focus on his breath for awhile, breathing deeply and slowly yet naturally. Have him count down from 10 to 1 slowly, feeling himself drift into a deeper, more relaxed state of being with each count.

When he is very deeply relaxed, have him picture or imagine a bright color, any color he wishes (have him take the first color that comes to him). Ask him to picture it as a sphere of bright light about six inches in diameter. Now ask him to picture it gradually growing bigger and bigger, until eventually it fills his whole field of mental vision. When he has experienced this, ask him to picture it shrinking, growing smaller and smaller, until it's back to its original size. Now have it grow smaller still, until it's only an inch or so in diameter, still shrinking, and finally disappearing completely.

Now go through the visualization exercise again, and this time have the person imagine that the color is his pain.

Invocation

To invoke means to "call in" or "call upon." Invocation used in meditation is a technique with which you can summon any type of energy or quality to come to you:

Close your eyes and relax deeply. Do some type of preparatory meditation such as grounding and running energy, or opening the energy centers, or simply going to your sanctuary, relaxing and breathing deeply for awhile.

When you feel relaxed and energized, say to yourself silently, yet firmly and clearly, "I now call forth the quality of love." Feel the energy of love coming to you, or coming out from someplace inside of you, filling you up, and radiating out from you. Remain for a few minutes totally experiencing the feeling. Then if you wish, direct it toward any particular goal through visualization and affirmation.

You can use the power of invocation to summon any quality or energy that you want or need . . .

strength	*warmth*
wisdom	*clarity*
serenity	*intelligence*
compassion	*creativity*
softness	*healing power* . . .

Simply make a strong, clear statement to yourself that this quality is now coming to you.

Another wonderful way to use the power of invocation is to summon the spirit or essence of a particular person who has qualities that you desire. If you invoke one of the masters, such as Buddha, Christ, or Mary, you are calling forth the universal qualities which that person symbolizes, which also lie within each of us. For example, if you call for Christ to work in you and through you, you are summoning in a very powerful way your own qualities of love, compassion, forgiveness, and healing ability.

If there is any particular master or teacher or hero with whom you resonate, call upon him or her through invocation whenever you feel the need to manifest his special qualities within yourself.

This type of meditation works beautifully when there is a special skill or talent that you wish to cultivate. For example, if you are studying music or art, call upon any great master in these fields whom you especially admire; picture him supporting and helping you, and feel his creative energy and genius flowing through you. It is not necessary to incorporate any personal problems or weaknesses he may have had; you are summoning him in his *highest aspect.* Many amazing results can be achieved through this meditation.

Ways to Use Affirmations

There are so many ways that affirmations can be used powerfully and effectively to give you a more positive, creative outlook and to help you achieve specific goals.

Remember, it's important to feel *relaxed* as you affirm. Do not be addicted to getting results. Remember that you already *are* everything you need; every improvement is just icing on the cake.

In meditation

1. Say them to yourself silently while meditating or relaxing deeply, especially right before going to sleep or right after waking up.

Spoken

1. Say them to yourself silently or aloud throughout the day, whenever you think of it, especially while driving, doing housework, or other routine tasks.

2. Say them to yourself aloud while looking at yourself in the mirror. This is especially good for affirmations to improve your self-esteem and self-love. Look yourself right in the eyes and affirm your beauty, lovableness, and worthiness. If you feel uncomfortable, stick with it until you push through those barriers and are able to fully experience looking at yourself and loving yourself. You may find that some emotion arises and is released through this process.

3. Record your affirmations on a tape recorder and play them to yourself around the house, while driving, etc. Use your name, and try doing them in the first, second, and third persons. For example, *"I, Shakti, am always deeply relaxed and centered in myself." "Shakti, you are always deeply relaxed and centered in yourself." "Shakti is always deeply relaxed and centered in herself."*

Or you can record a little speech, maybe three or four paragraphs long, describing your ideal visualization of yourself or a particular situation. This also can be done in the first, second, and/or third person.

Written

1. Take a particular affirmation and write it out 10 or 20 times in succession, *really thinking* about the words as you write them. Change the affirmation as you go along if you think of better ways to say it. This is one of the most powerful techniques I've ever found, and one of the easiest to do. I've devoted a chapter to it in Section Four.

2. Write or type out affirmations and paste them up in various places around your house or at your job as reminders. Good places are: on the refrigerator, your phone, your mirror, your desk, over your bed, on the dining table.

With others

1. If you have a friend who wants to work on affirmations as well, you can do them very effectively in partners. Sit facing each other, look into each other's eyes, and take turns saying affirmations to each other and accepting them.

David: "Linda, you are a beautiful, loving, and creative person."

Linda: "Yes, I know!"

Repeat this 10 or 15 times the same way, then switch partners so that Linda says the affirmation to David and he agrees with it. Then try it in the first person:

David: "*I, David, am a beautiful, loving, and creative person.*"

Linda: "*Yes, you certainly are.*"

Repeat several times.

Be sure to say the affirmations sincerely and meaningfully, even if you feel a little silly at first. It's a wonderful opportunity to outflow love and support to another person, and to really support them in changing their negative concepts to positive ones.

It's practically guaranteed that after doing this process together you will be experiencing a deep love space together . . .

2. In a more informal way, ask your friends to say affirmations to you frequently. For example, if you want to affirm that you are learning to express yourself more easily, you might ask a good friend to say to you often, "*Jeannie, you are certainly speaking out and expressing yourself clearly these days!*"

Make a game out of doing this for each other and you will find it helpful. We automatically tend to give a lot of power to what our friends say to us, for good or bad; our minds tend to accept what others tell us about ourselves. So getting strong positive feedback from friends in the form of affirmations really works.

3. Begin to include affirmations in your conversations— making strong positive statements about things and people (including yourself) that you want to see in a more positive way. It's amazing what dramatic changes can be made in your life by just beginning to consciously speak more positively in daily conversation.

A word of caution: *do not* use this technique in such a way that you feel like you are contradicting your true feelings. Do not use it when you are feeling upset or strongly negative or it will feel like you are repressing yourself. Use it from a constructive space, to help change your unconscious negative speech patterns and underlying assumptions.

Singing and chanting

1. Make a point of learning songs that affirm the reality you would like to create for yourself; listen to them and sing them often. A large part of our present consciousness has been formed by popular music which creates a reality in which we feel hopelessly dependent on our lover, would die if he left us, wonder if life is worth living if we can't "have" a certain person, and so on.

In my recommended reading list I've mentioned a few records and music tapes which consciously come from a different point of view.

2. Make up your own songs or simple chants using the affirmations you want to work with.

More affirmations

Accepting Ourselves

I accept myself completely here and now.
I love myself completely as I am, and I'm getting better all the time.
I accept all my feelings as part of myself.
I'm beautiful and loveable however I'm feeling.
I am now willing to experience all my feelings.
It's good to express my feelings. I now give myself permission to express my feelings.
I love myself when I express my feelings.

Feeling Good

It's okay for me to have fun and enjoy myself and I do!
I like to do things that make me feel good.
I am always deeply relaxed and centered.
I now feel deep inner peace and serenity.
I'm glad I was born and I love being alive.

Relationships

I love myself and I naturally attract loving relationships into my life.
I am strong and loving in my relationships.
I deserve love and sexual pleasure.
I am now ready to accept a happy, fulfilling relationship.

I am now ready for all my relationships to work.
The more I love myself the more I love _____.
I love _____ *and* _____ *loves me.*
All difficulties between me and _____ *are now being dissolved. We have a wonderful relationship.*
Divine love is working through me now to create a perfect relationship with _____.
I am now attracting exactly the kind of relationship I want.
I am now divinely irresistible to my perfect mate.

Opening Creativity

I am now an open channel for creative energy.
Creative ideas and inspiration are coming to me every day.
I am the creator of my life.
I am now creating my life exactly as I want it.

Divine Love and Guidance

Divine love is doing its perfect work in this situation now for the good of all concerned.
Divine love and light are working through me now.
Divine love goes before me and prepares the way.
God is showing me the way now.
My inner wisdom is guiding me now.
I am now being guided to the perfect solution to this problem.
The light within me is creating miracles in my body, mind, and affairs, here and now.

Part Four

Special Techniques

If you would learn the secret of right relations
look only for the divine in people and things,
and leave all the rest to God.

J. Allen Boone
in *Kinship With All Life*

A Creative Visualization Notebook

It's a very good idea to start a notebook which can serve as your creative visualization workbook. In this section I will be giving you a number of written exercises and processes which you might want to do and keep in your notebook. You may wish to write down affirmations that you hear or think of, so that you can refer to them when you need them. There are many other creative ways to use your notebook, such as recording your dreams and fantasies, keeping a journal of your progress with creative visualization, writing down inspiring thoughts and ideas, or quotes from books and songs that are meaningful to you, drawing pictures or writing your own poems and songs that express your expanding awareness.

I have a notebook in which I regularly work on my goals, affirmations, ideal scenes, and treasure maps, and I have found it a very valuable tool in the transformation of my life.

Here are a few suggestions for starting your notebook:

1. Affirmations. Write down your favorite affirmations. You can list them all on one page, or you might want to make a separate page for each, with decorative borders and designs, so that each time you read through it you have a beautiful experience as you pause and meditate on each one.

2. Outflow List. Make a list of all the ways that you can outflow your energy to the world and to others around you, both generally and specifically. Include ways that you outflow money, time, love and affection, appreciation, physical energy, friendship, touching, and your special talents and abilities. Add to this list anytime you think of new things.

3. Success List. Make a list of everything you feel you are a success at, or have been a success at, or have done successfully at some time in your life. Include things in all areas of your life, not just your work. Write down everything that has meaning for you, even if it might not to someone else. Keep adding to it as you think of more things, or accomplish new successes. The purpose of this list is to acknowledge yourself and your abilities, which gives you added energy for accomplishing more.

4. Appreciation List. Make a list of everything you can think of that you are especially thankful for, or that you especially appreciate having in your life. Making and adding to this list can really open up your heart, and your awareness of the many riches we all have in our lives that we often take for granted. It increases your realization of prosperity and abundance on every level, and thus your ability to manifest.

5. Self-Esteem List. Make a list of all the things you like about yourself, all your positive qualities. This is not an "ego trip"—the better you feel about yourself and the more you acknowledge your own wonderful qualities, the happier and more loving you will be, the more your creative energy will flow, and the greater contribution you will make to the world.

6. Self-Appreciation List. Write down all the ways you can think of to be good to yourself, nice things that you can do for yourself, things that are just for your own pleasure and satisfaction. They can be small or large, but make some of them things you can easily do every day, and then do them! This increases your sense of well-being and satisfaction in life, which in turn helps you to come from a clearer space in creating your life.

7. Healing and Assistance List. Write down the names of any people you know who need healing, or special support and assistance of any sort. Write down special affirmations for them. Every time you look through your notebook you will be giving them a special boost of your energy.

8. Fantasies and Creative Ideas. Jot down any ideas, plans, or dreams for the future, or any creative ideas that come to you, even if they seem farfetched, or you're sure you'll never follow through on them. This will help to loosen you up and stimulate your imagination and your natural creative ability.

You may find it difficult to take time out of your busy schedule to work in your notebook. Yet if you take a few minutes a day, or an hour or two every week or so, you will find that so much work is accomplished on the inner plane, it is often worth a hundred times the amount of time and energy you would have spent on the outer plane.

Clearing

In learning to use creative visualization you may get in touch with blocks in yourself that hold you back from attaining your highest good.

A "block" is a place where energy is constricted—not moving, not flowing. Usually blocks are caused initially by repressed emotions of fear, guilt, and/or resentment (anger) which cause a person to tighten up and close down spiritually, emotionally, mentally and even physically.

In dealing with a block on any level, what's needed is to get energy moving and flowing in that area. The keys to this are:

1. Mental and emotional acceptance (on a physical level this manifests as relaxation and release).

2. Clear observation, which leads to understanding of the root of the problem—which is always a limiting attitude or belief.

So in dealing with an area of consciousness where we have a block, we need to first experience (as fully as possible) the emotion we have locked up in that area, in a loving, accepting way. In doing so, we get the blocked up energy moving and we have a chance to observe the underlying negative beliefs or attitudes which caused the problem to begin with. We can take a good clear look at them and let them dissolve themselves.

Amazingly enough, it seems to be the process of pinpointing the constrictive belief and accepting the feelings you have around it which works magic; the difficulty almost inevitably dissolves and disappears eventually once you've understood and accepted yourself. It's much simpler than you may think.

The trick is to simultaneously *love and accept yourself* compassionately for having this belief, and at the same time to *see clearly that you are ready to let go of it* because it is limiting, destructive, self-defeating and *untrue*.

Some common core beliefs that are most prevalent and troublesome are:

I'm not okay . . . there's something wrong with me . . . I'm unworthy and undeserving.

I've done bad things (or a bad thing) in my life and I deserve to suffer (be punished) for it.

People (including me) are basically bad—selfish, cruel, stupid, untrustworthy, foolish, etc.

The world is an unsafe place.

There's not enough _____ *(love, money, good things, etc.) to go around, so:*

> *I have to struggle to get my share*
>
> *or*
>
> *It's hopeless, I'll never get enough*
>
> *or*
>
> *If I have a lot, someone else will have to do without.*

Life is painful, suffering, hard work . . . it's not meant to be fun.

Love is dangerous . . . I might get hurt.

Power is dangerous . . . I might hurt someone.

Money is the root of all evil. Money corrupts.

The world doesn't work and never will. In fact it's getting worse all the time.

I don't have control over what happens to me . . . I'm powerless to do anything about my life or the state of the world.

As you read through these negative ideas, see whether any of them reflect an underlying assumption of your own belief system or emotional pattern.

Depressing though they may seem when you read through them all at once, the fact is that every one of us has bought into some of these (or other) negative viewpoints about reality, at least in some degree. If we hadn't, we would all be manifesting as fully realized beings, as it is only the degree to which we accept these beliefs that separates us from realization of our God-like nature.

And it's no wonder that we have incorporated these ideas into our sense of reality—they are all extremely prevalent in our world at this time in our evolution. In fact, the world is currently being run according to these ideas, although fortunately this is rapidly changing.

The important thing to realize is that they are only *beliefs*; they have no objective truth. Although they may *seem* to be true at times when we look around us, that is only because so many human beings believe them and act accordingly.

The most powerful thing you can do (and it is very powerful) to change the world, is to change your own beliefs about the nature of life, people, reality, to something more positive . . . and begin to act accordingly.

This book will give you some tools to do so.

Clearing exercises:
If you are having trouble realizing a goal, or sense resistance in yourself to its achievement, try this exercise:

1. Take a piece of paper and write at the top, "The reason I can't have what I want is . . .", then immediately begin to write a list of any thoughts that come into your head to complete the sentence. Don't take too much time and don't

*take it too seriously, just quickly write down about 20 or 30
things that come to you even if they seem silly or stupid. A
sample list might start like this:*
The reason I can't have what I want is . . .

> *I'm too lazy*
> *I don't have enough money*
> *It doesn't exist*
> *I've tried before and it never worked*
> *Mother said I couldn't*
> *I don't want to*
> *It's too hard*
> *I'm afraid to*
> *John wouldn't like it*
> *It's too much fun*
> *and so on . . .*

2. *Try the same exercise, only this time specifically name
the thing that you want, i.e. "The reason I can't have a good
job is . . ." and proceed as before.*
*Now just sit quietly for a few minutes with your list and
see whether any of the thoughts you've written down ring
true for you . . . whether in some way or degree you believe
them. Just get a sense of what kind of limitations you put on
yourself and your world.*

3. *Now write a list of all the most negative attitudes you
can think of about yourself, other people, relationships, the
world, life.*
*Again, sit quietly with your list and get in touch with
which of these ideas may consciously or unconsciously hold
emotional power over you.*

If at any point in any of these exercises you feel
emotions coming up, just stay with that and allow
yourself to experience it as much as possible, with total
acceptance. You may get a flash of an early experience,
or something your parents or teachers used to tell you
which programmed your view of the world in a certain
way.

4. *Whenever you feel complete with this process, especially if you've gotten in touch with one or more negative beliefs that you hold, simply tear up your lists and throw them away. This symbolizes how little power they actually need to have in your life.*

Then sit quietly, relax, and do some affirmations to replace your constricted, limiting beliefs with more opening, constructive, positive ones.

A few possible clearing affirmations:

I now release my entire past, It is complete and I am free!
I now dissolve all negative, limiting beliefs. They have no power over me!
I now forgive and release everyone in my life. We are all happy and free.
I don't have to try to please others. I am naturally lovable and likeable no matter what I do!
I now let go of all accumulated guilt, fears, resentment, disappointments, and grudges. I am free and clear!
All of my negative self-images and attitudes are now dissolved. I love and appreciate myself!
All barriers to my full expression and enjoyment of life are now dissolved.
The world is a beautiful place to be.
The universe always provides.

More clearing exercises:

1. *Forgiveness and release.* Write down on a piece of paper the names of everyone in your life whom you feel has ever mistreated you, harmed you, done you an injustice, or toward whom you feel or have felt resentment, hurt or anger. Next to each person's name write down what they did to you, or what you resent them for.

Then close your eyes, relax, and one by one visualize or imagine each person. Hold a little conversation with each one, and explain to him or her that in the past you have felt anger or hurt toward them, but that now you are going to do your best to forgive them for everything, and to dissolve and release all constricted energy between you. Give them a bless-

*ing and say, "I forgive you and release you. Go your own
way and be happy."*

*When you have finished this process, write on your paper
"I now forgive you and release you all" and throw it away,
as a symbol that you are letting go of these past experiences.*

Many people find that this process of forgiveness and
release is miraculous in relieving them immediately of
their long-standing burdens of accumulated resentment
and hostility. The wonderful thing is that the other
people involved, even if you never see them again, will
on a psychic level pick up your forgiveness and it will
help to clear up their lives as well.

It may be that the first time you do this process you
will not have an experience of relief and release with
certain people (especially a parent, spouse or other
very significant person in your life). If not, continue to
do the process from time to time, continue blessing
and forgiving them as much as you can find it in your
heart to do so, and eventually it will be resolved for
you. (Remember it is for your *own* benefit, health and
happiness that you are doing this.)*

Many people experience miraculous healing of physical problems after doing this process, as many physical ailments such as cancer and arthritis are directly
related to accumulated anger and resentment.

2. *Now write down everyone you can think of in your life
whom you feel you have hurt or done an injustice, and write
down what you did to them.*

*Again close your eyes, relax, and imagine each person in
turn. Tell him or her what you did, and ask them to forgive
you and give you their blessing. Then picture them doing so.*

*When you have finished the process, write at the bottom of
your paper (or across the whole thing) "I forgive myself and
absolve myself of all guilt, here and now, and forever!" Then
tear up the paper and throw it away.*

* I recommend reading Catherine Ponder's *The Prospering
Power of Love.*

One final clearing process:
Go through your closets, drawers, basement, garage, or desk—wherever you have accumulated "stuff" that you don't need, and throw it out or give it away.

This vigorous, concrete action on the physical level is symbolic of what you are doing on mental, emotional and psychic levels—clearing out old, useless stuff, getting the energy flow moving, and getting your "house in order." It will make you feel great, especially if you do affirmations while you're doing it, such as:

"The more I outflow, the more space I create for good things to come to me."

"I love giving and I love receiving."

"As I clean up and clear out my physical space I am cleaning up and clearing out my life in every way."

"I am now putting my life in order, preparing to accept all the good that is coming to me now."

"I give thanks now for all the good that I have and all the good things to come."

Writing Affirmations

The technique I'm about to describe has brought some of the fastest and most dramatic changes in my life on many different occasions. It is a combination of writing affirmations and a clearing process, neatly rolled into one. I love it because it is so simple and easy to do, yet it gets down to a very deep level.

Writing affirmations is a very dynamic technique because the written word has so much power over our minds. We are both writing and reading them at the same time, so it's like a double hit of energy.

Take any affirmation you want to work with and write it 10 or 20 times in succession on a piece of paper. Use your name, and try writing it in the first, second, and third persons. (For example: I, John, am a gifted singer and songwriter. John, you are a gifted singer and songwriter. John is a gifted singer and songwriter.)

Don't just write it by rote; really think about the meaning of the words as you are writing them. Notice whether you feel any resistance, doubts, or negative thoughts about what you are writing. Whenever you do (even a slight one) turn the paper over, and on the back write out the negative thought, the reason why the affirmation can't be true, can't work, or whatever. (For example: "I'm really not good enough" "I'm too old" "This isn't going to work.") Then go back to writing the affirmation.

When you are finished, take a look at the back of the paper. If you have been honest, you will have a good look at the reasons why you keep yourself from having what you want in this particular case.

With this in mind, think of some affirmations you can do to help you counteract these negative fears or beliefs, and begin to write out these new affirmations. Or you may want to stick with the original affirmation if it seems effective, or modify it slightly to be more accurate.

Keep working with writing the affirmations once or twice a day for a few days. Once you feel that you've really looked at your negative programming, discontinue writing it out, and just keep writing the affirmations.

My experience with this process is that whatever I have been affirming often manifests within a matter of a few days or even a few hours. And I have usually gotten many valuable insights into my own patterns this way.

Setting Goals

Possibly the trickiest part of getting what you want in life is just figuring out what you really want! And yet it is certainly the most important part of all.

I have found this to be unfailingly true in my life: As soon as I have a very clear, strong intention to create a particular thing, it manifests almost immediately (often within hours or days of getting clear about it) with very little effort involved. I experience this as a kind of "click" in my consciousness, when I suddenly get a very strong experience of what I want, and an equally strong experience that I'm going to get it . . . It usually takes a certain amount of time and energy spent in processing before I arrive at that point of clarity. And very often the "click of clarity" has been preceded by feelings of confusion, despair, hopelessness and so on, which I have had to work my way through. So don't worry . . . the darkest hour is truly just before the dawn.

Discovering what you want in your life can be facilitated by the process of setting goals. I often find it helpful to do some exercises with pen and paper, which I will share with you. When you are working on setting goals it's important to keep a few things in mind.

Remember that setting goals does *not* mean that you are stuck with those goals. You can change them as often as you want to and feel that it's necessary.

Remember also that setting goals does *not* mean that you have to pursue them through effort, striving or struggling. It does not mean that you have to become emotionally addicted to achieving them. On the contrary, setting goals can help you flow through life more easily, effortlessly and pleasurably. The nature of life is movement and creativity, and goals give you a clear focus and direction in which to channel your natural creative energy, thereby helping you to outflow and contribute to the world, which enhances your feeling of well-being and satisfaction in life. Goals are there to help you and support you in your true purpose.

Goals can be made in the spirit that life is an enjoyable game to be played, and one that can be deeply rewarding. They are not to be taken too heavily or seriously. At the same time, you must give them enough weight and importance so that they are of real value to you.

You may find that the very process of choosing goals will bring up a certain amount of emotional resistance in you. You might experience this in various different ways, such as feeling depressed, hopeless, or overwhelmed at the thought of trying to set goals. Or you might feel the desire to distract yourself by eating, sleeping, or whatever. These emotional reactions (if you should have them) are clues to the ways in which you avoid getting what you want in life. It's important to go ahead and experience these feelings and reactions, to go through them and proceed with the process. Once you get into it you will find it of value.

Then again, you may thoroughly enjoy the whole process and find it very expansive, fun and enlightening. I hope so!

Don't make the choosing of goals too complicated or significant. Start with simple, obvious things. Remember you can always change and develop them as you go along.

Exercises:
1. *Sit down with a pen and paper and write down the following categories:*

Work/career
Money
Life style/possessions
Relationships
Creative self-expression
Leisure/travel
Personal growth/education

Now, keeping in mind your present life situation, write down under each category some things that you would like to have, to change, or to improve in the near future. Don't think too hard about it, simply write down any ideas that come to your mind as good possibilities.

The purpose of this exercise is to loosen you up and get you thinking about what you want in the various areas of your life.

2. Take another piece of paper and write at the top: "If I could be, do, and have everything I want, this would be my ideal scene:"

Now list the same seven categories, and after each one, write a paragraph or two (or however much you want!) describing your absolute ideal situation in life, as far as you can fantasize about it.

The purpose of this exercise is to stretch and expand you beyond your present limits, so let your imagination take over, and really let yourself have everything you could ever want.

When you have finished this, add one more category—world situation/environment. Describe the kinds of changes you would like to see happen in the world in your lifetime, if you could have the power to change things—world peace, the end of poverty, people becoming conscious of each other and the earth, schools transformed into exciting learning centers, hospitals becoming true centers of healing, and so on. You can be as creative as you like with this category, and you may find that you have all kinds of interesting ideas you never thought of before.

Now re-read the whole thing and meditate on it awhile. Create a mental picture for yourself of a wonderful life in a beautiful world.

3. *Again, take a fresh sheet of paper. Based on what seems most meaningful from the ideal scene you have created above, write a list of the ten or twelve most important goals for your life, as you feel them to be right now. Remember you can change and revise this list at any time (and you should do so from time to time).*

4. *Now write down: My Five Year Goals, and list the most important goals you would like to achieve within the next five years.*

It's great to write your goals in the form of affirmations, as if they had already been achieved. This helps to achieve a clearer, stronger effect. For example:

I now own 20 acres of land in the country, with a beautiful house, orchards, a creek, and lots of animals.

I now support myself easily and abundantly through singing and playing my own songs for enthusiastic and appreciative audiences.

In writing your goals, be sure to put down things that are real and meaningful to you, things that you actually want, *not* what you think you *should want*. No one else need ever see your goals unless you want them to, and this process requires that you be totally honest with yourself.

5. *Repeat the process above with your goals for one year. Don't make too many; if you have a lot at first, eliminate all but the five or six most important ones. Check to see that they are in alignment with your five year goals. That is, make sure they are moving in the same general direction so that when you accomplish your one year goals, you will be a step closer to your five year goals. For example, if one of your five year goals is to own your own business, one of your one year goals might be to have a certain amount of money saved toward that end, or to have a job in a similar business where you are getting a certain type of experience you will need.*

Now write out your goals for six months from now, one month, and one week from now. Again, keep it simple and choose the three or four that are most important. Be realistic about how much you can accomplish in the shorter range goals. Again make sure they are in alignment with your longer range goals.

You may find it difficult to be so specific about events so far in the future, and you may have an uncomfortable feeling about planning your life ahead. However, just making a plan does not oblige you to follow it; in fact you are bound to change considerably. This exercise is for the purpose of:

a) getting practice in setting goals,
b) acknowledging that some of your fantasies *can* become reality if you wish them to, and
c) getting in touch with some of the important purposes and directions in your life.

I suggest that you keep your goals in your notebook. Every now and then, perhaps every month or so, or whenever it feels like a helpful thing to do, sit down with your notebook and do some of the processes again, revising and reshaping your goals as needed. Be sure to date your paper each time you do this, and keep them in order in your notebook, as it is very interesting and informative to look back and see how they gradually evolve.

Some general rules:

1. For short range goals (one week, one month) be fairly simple and realistic—choose things that you are pretty sure you can accomplish, unless you especially feel like taking on a big challenge (which can be very good sometimes too). The further range your goal, the more expansive and imaginative you can be, so that your horizons are constantly extended.

2. When you find that you have not accomplished some of your goals (which will inevitably happen) do not criticize yourself or assume that you have failed. Simply acknowledge clearly to yourself that you have not accomplished that goal, and decide whether it is still a goal for you; that is, decide whether you want to set it again for yourself, or whether you want to let it go. It is *most* important that you acknowledge unac-

complished goals in this way. Otherwise, they may accumulate in the back of your mind and you will feel unconsciously that you have "failed," which will eventually make you tend to avoid goal setting.

3. When you find that you *have* accomplished a goal, even a small one, be sure to acknowledge yourself for that. Give yourself a pat on the back and enjoy at least a moment of satisfaction about it. All too often, we accomplish our goals, and forget to even notice or enjoy the fact that we have done so!

4. Don't take on too much at once. Set goals that feel good to you. If you feel overwhelmed, confused, or discouraged . . . simplify. You may want to work on goals in one area of your life only, such as your job or your relationships. This process is ultimately to help you enjoy your life more.

If you set a lot of goals that you don't accomplish you are probably either setting them unrealistically high, or setting goals that you don't truly desire and therefore have no real inner intention of pursuing. Choose goals that you genuinely like and want.

Your goals should make you feel *good*—uplifted, expanded, pleasured, challenged. If not, find ones that do!

Ideal Scene

Creative visualization can take the form of mental imagery and words, of spoken words (affirmations), of written words, or of a physical image or picture (treasure map). Anything that helps you to create a clear "blue print" to put out in the universe is an aid in creative visualization.

This exercise will help you to create a clear picture through written words. The process of doing it will help you get clearer about what you really want, and it will help you to manifest it. I use it for all my important goals.

Exercise:
Think of a goal that is important to you. It can be a long range or short range one.

Write down the goal as clearly as possible in one sentence.

Underneath that, write Ideal Scene, *and proceed to describe the situation exactly as you would like it to be when your goal is fully realized. Describe it in the present tense, as if it already exists, in as much detail as you wish.*

When you have finished, write at the bottom,

"This or something better is now manifesting for me in totally satisfying and harmonious ways,"
and add any other affirmations you wish, and sign your name.

Then sit quietly, relax, visualize your ideal scene at your meditational level of mind, and do your affirmations.

Keep your ideal scene in your notebook, in your desk, near your bed, or hang it on your wall. Read it often, and make appropriate changes when necessary. Bring it to mind during your meditation periods.

One word of warning . . . if you put it away in a drawer and forget about it, you are very likely to find one day that it has manifested anyhow . . . without your consciously putting any energy into it at all.

I have often looked back through my old goals, ideal scenes, and treasure maps, surprised to find that things I had completely forgotten have magically come into being in my life, almost exactly as I had originally pictured them.

Treasure Maps

Making a "treasure map" is a very powerful technique, and fun to do.

A treasure map is an actual, physical picture of your desired reality. It is valuable because it forms an especially clear, sharp image which can then attract and focus energy into your goal. It works along the same lines as a blueprint for a building.

You can make a treasure map by drawing or painting it, or by making a collage using pictures and words cut from magazines, books, or cards, photographs, lettering, drawing and so on. Don't worry if you're not artistically accomplished. Simple, childlike treasure maps are just as effective as great works of art!

Basically the treasure map should show you in your ideal scene, with your goal fully realized.

Here are some guidelines that will help you make the most effective treasure maps:

1. Do a treasure map for a single goal or area of your life, so that you can be sure to include all the elements without getting too complicated. This enables the mind to focus on it more clearly and easily than if you include all your goals on one treasure map. You might want to do one treasure map for your relationships, one for your job, one for your spiritual growth, and so on.

2. You can make it any size that's convenient for you. You may want to keep it in your notebook, hang it on your wall, or carry it in your pocket or purse. I usually make mine on light cardboard which holds up better than paper.

3. Be sure to put yourself in the picture. For a very realistic effect, use a photograph of yourself. Otherwise draw yourself in. Show yourself being, doing, or having your desired objective—traveling around the world, wearing your new clothes, proud author of your new book, etc.

4. Show the situation in its ideal, complete form, as if it already exists. You don't need to indicate *how* it's going to come about. This is the finished product. Don't show anything negative or undesirable.

5. Use lots of color in your treasure map to increase the power and impact on your consciousness.

6. Show yourself in a real setting; make it look believable to yourself.

7. Include some symbol of the infinite which has meaning and power for you. It could be an "om" sign, a cross, Christ, a Buddha, a sun radiating light or anything that represents universal intelligence or God. This is an acknowledgement and a reminder that everything comes from the infinite source.

8. Put affirmations on your treasure map. *"Here I am driving my new Datsun truck with a camper top. I love it, and I have plenty of money to maintain it."*

Be sure to include also the cosmic affirmation *"This or something better now manifests for me in totally satisfying and harmonious ways for all concerned."*

The process of creating your treasure map is a powerful step toward manifesting your goal. Now just spend a few minutes each day quietly looking at it, and every once in a while throughout the day give it a thought. That is all that's necessary.

Some Sample Ideas for Treasure Maps
To stimulate your imagination, here are a few possible ideas for treasure maps:

Health: Show yourself radiantly healthy, active, beautiful, participating in whatever activities would indicate perfect health.

Weight or physical condition: Show yourself with your perfect body (cut a picture from a magazine that looks like *you* would look in your perfect condition, and paste a photo of your head on the body!), feeling wonderful about yourself. You can make statements with balloons around them coming out of your mouth like in cartoons, to indicate how you are feeling, i.e., *"I feel wonderful and look fantastic now that I weigh 125 lbs. and am in great physical condition."*

Self-image and beauty: Show yourself as you want to feel about yourself . . . beautiful, relaxed, enjoying life, warm and loving. Include words and symbols that represent these qualities to you.

Relationships: Put photos of yourself and your friend, lover, husband, wife or child in your treasure map, with pictures, symbols, and affirmations showing that you are happy, loving, communicating, enjoying a deep, wonderful sexual relationship, and so on.

If you are looking for a new relationship find pictures and words that represent qualities you desire in the person and the relationship; show yourself with the ideal person for you.

Job or career: Show yourself doing what you really want to do, with interesting, agreeable co-workers, earning plenty of money (be specific about how much you want), in the location you desire, and any other pertinent details.

Creativity: Use symbols, colors, and pictures that indicate your creativity is really opening up. Show yourself doing and manifesting creative, beautiful, interesting things and feeling great about it.

Family and friends: Show members of your family or friends in totally harmonious, loving relationships with you and each other.

Travel: Show yourself wherever you want to be, with plenty of time and money to enjoy it.

And so on. You get the idea. Have fun!

Health and Beauty

There are so many ways that creative visualization can be used to maintain and improve our health, physical fitness and beauty. Like everything else, our health and attractiveness are created by our mental attitudes, so changing our beliefs and the way we tune into ourselves and the world can have profound physical effects.

I have already mentioned the value of doing treasure maps in these areas. Here are a few other techniques that I like to use. I'm sure you'll find many more of your own.

Physical exercise
No matter what type of physical exercise you do, you can use creative visualization and affirmation to help you get maximum benefit and enjoyment from it. You can use visualization both while you are doing the physical exercise, and also at other times, while sitting in meditation or relaxing.

For example, if you like to run, picture yourself running very swiftly, smoothly, and tirelessly. While you are running, imagine that you are taking a huge leap with every step, covering vast territory effortlessly, almost flying. During relaxation periods, affirm to yourself that you are daily growing faster, stronger, and in better physical shape. Picture yourself winning races, if that is one of your goals.

If you do dance or yoga exercises, while you are doing them put your consciousness in your body, in your muscles, picture them relaxing and stretching, see yourself becoming more and more limber and flexible.

Use creative visualization to improve your abilities in your favorite sport; imagine yourself becoming more and more accomplished until you are truly excelling.

Beauty treatments

Do things for yourself regularly that make you feel that you are taking special care of yourself and doing nice things for your body. Using creative visualization can turn a daily routine into a beauty treatment ritual.

For example, take a hot bath or shower, and visualize the hot water totally relaxing, soothing, and healing you. Picture any problems melting or being washed away, and nothing remaining but your natural radiance, shining from within.

Put lotion or oil on your face and body, giving yourself lots of loving attention, affirming that your skin is becoming smoother and more beautiful all the time. When you wash your hair, put your attention in what you're doing, and affirm that your hair is thicker, shinier, and healthier than ever before. When you brush your teeth, mentally affirm that they are strong, healthy, and beautiful. And so on.

Eating rituals

Many people have negative concepts relating to food. We are afraid the food we eat is going to make us fat, or make us sick (unhealthy). Yet we tend to compulsively continue eating the very foods we fear, thus creating inner stress and conflict, and eventually creating the feared effects—fatness and illness.

Also, many people are very unconscious while they eat. We are so busy talking and thinking of other things, we fail to tune in to the delicious, satisfying taste and nutrition of our food.

Eating is really a magic ritual, an amazing process in which various forms of energy from the universe are transformed into the energy that forms our bodies. Whatever we are thinking and feeling at the time is part of the alchemy.

Here is a ritual to practice at least once a day if possible, no matter what you are eating:

Sit down with your food in front of you. Close your eyes for a moment, relax, and take a deep breath. Silently thank the universe for this food, and thank all the beings who helped provide it, including the plants and animals, the people who grew it and prepared it for you.

Open your eyes and look at the food; really observe what it looks like. Observe how it smells. Slowly begin to eat it; really be aware of and enjoy the taste. As you are eating, talk to yourself silently in your mind, and tell yourself that this food is being transformed into life energy for your use. Tell yourself that your body is using everything that it needs, and easily eliminating anything that it doesn't need. Picture yourself becoming healthier and more beau-tiful as a result of eating the food. Do this regardless of any other previous concepts you may have of how good or bad the food is for you.

If possible, eat slowly, and take a moment or two after you finish to enjoy the pleasant warm glow that emanates from your stomach when it is satisfied and happy.

The more often you remember to tune into your food this way, the more beauty and good health you will create for yourself.

Here is another ritual that is even simpler:

Before going to bed, when you arise, or sometime during the day pour yourself a tall glass of cool water. Sit down, relax, and drink it slowly. As you drink, tell yourself that this water is the elixir of life and the fountain of youth. Imagine that it is washing away all impurities and bringing you energy, vitality, beauty and health.

Here are some good affirmations for health and beauty:

Every day I am growing more beautiful and more radiantly healthy!

Everything I do adds to my health and beauty.

Everything I eat adds to my health, beauty, and slender attractiveness.

I am good to my body, and my body is good to me.

I am now slender, strong, and in perfect condition no matter what I do.

I am growing stronger and more powerful every day.

I now desire to eat only those things that are best for me at any given time.

The more I love and appreciate myself, the more beautiful I am becoming.

I am now irresistibly attractive to men (or women).

Creative Visualization in Groups

Many of the techniques that I have given in this book can be easily adapted for use in groups. Creative visualization is especially good when used by a group, because the group energy automatically gives it a lot of power. Each person's energy tends to support the others, and in this case the whole becomes more than the sum of its parts.

No matter what the group you are involved in, whether it is your family or a group of friends, a work group, social action group, church or spiritual group, or a workshop or class, you may find that creative visualization provides you with tools for achieving your group's goals, or just for tuning into each other in a deeper way.

Here are some of the ways you can use creative visualization in a group:

Singing and chanting. Choose songs or chants that express a feeling, an idea, or an attitude that you want to create or cultivate in yourselves and in the world. Music is very powerful in effecting change.

Meditating and imaging. Choose a goal or image, and have everyone sit in silent meditation, visualizing and affirming it together. You may be amazed at the results.

114

Treasure mapping. Have each person create their own treasure map for a group goal, or as a group create one treasure map together. Or you can even appoint a committee to make a treasure map!

Affirmations. Do affirmations in partners, as I described in the section on how to use affirmations. Or have the whole group speak affirmations aloud together.

Healing. Healing in groups is a wonderful experience. See the section on healing meditations.

Creative Visualization
in Relationships

One of the most valuable ways we can use creative visualization is in improving our relationships. Because human beings are so sensitive to each other on so many levels, we are especially susceptible and receptive to the thought forms that we hold about each other. It is these thought forms and the underlying attitudes that they reflect which form our relationships, and cause them to work or not work.

In relationship, as in everything else, we get exactly what we believe in, expect, and "ask for" on our deepest levels. The people we are in relationship with are always a mirror, reflecting our own beliefs, and simultaneously we are mirrors, reflecting their beliefs. So relationship is one of the most powerful tools for growth that we have; if we look honestly at our relationships we can see so much about how we have created them.

Take an attitude of total responsibility about your relationship. Assume for a moment that you alone are responsible for creating it the way it is, no matter how much it may look to you like the other person is responsible for certain things. If there are certain things about the relationship that are unsatisfying to you, ask yourself why and how you have created it that way. See if you can discover what core beliefs you have that cause you to create a less than satisfying, happy, loving relationship. What is the payoff for you in keeping yourself in an unhappy space? (There is always a payoff in everything we do; otherwise we wouldn't do it.)

If you truly *desire* to have deeply fulfilling, happy relationships in your life, if you *believe* that it is possible for you to have them, and if you are willing to *accept* that happiness and satisfaction, then you can and will create relationships that work for you.

Here are some things you can do to help you with your relationships:

1. Look at your goals in the relationship. What do you truly want out of this relationship? Consider all levels—physical, emotional, mental, and spiritual. Write out an ideal scene, or do a treasure map that expresses your perfect visualization in this relationship.

2. Take a good honest look at what beliefs and attitudes are keeping you from creating what you want. You can use a clearing process to help you get in touch with your limiting attitudes. For example, you can write "The reason I can't have a perfect relationship with _____ is. . . ." or "The reason I can't have what I want in this relationship is. . . ." Then write all the responses that come up for you.

3. Use affirmation and visual imagery to change your negative beliefs, and to start visualizing and creating beautiful, loving, fulfilling relationships.

4. The technique of saying affirmations to each other can often help to improve relationships dramatically. Of course it's very important to communicate with each other honestly from your true feelings about what you like and don't like, and what you want. But instead of continuously complaining about each other's shortcomings and weaknesses, try making an agreement to *affirm* to each other that you are improving and making progress in your growth and development. So instead of "George, why do you always interrupt me when I'm

saying something" you might agree to say to George at appropriate moments "I appreciate the way you are becoming a good listener." In this way you not only remind George in a friendly way to be a better listener, but you also begin to change your image of George, as well as George's image of himself.

Remember that the potential for perfection lies within every relationship, just as it lies within each individual. It is already there, we simply have to uncover it by removing the layers of "stuff" we have put on top of it.

All too often in ongoing relationships we have gotten stuck in certain roles and images with each other which we find it difficult to change. It's as if we've put ourselves and each other in a certain box with certain labels on it. We find this very limiting and confining, but don't always know how to step out of it.

Creative visualization provides us with a wonderful tool for expanding out of our roles and stereotypes. Begin to visualize and affirm new images for yourself and for the other person; see the potential for positive change within every person and every situation, and give energy and support to that positive change through creative visualization.

Part Five

Living Creatively

*The only successful manifestation
is one which brings about a change
or growth in consciousness;
that is, it has manifested God,
or revealed him more fully,
as well as having manifested a form . . .*

David Spangler
in *Manifestation*

Creative Consciousness

Creative visualization is not just a technique, but ultimately it is a state of consciousness. It is a consciousness in which we deeply realize that we are the continuous creators of our universe and we take responsibility for that at all moments.

There is no separation between us and God; we are divine expressions of the creative principle on this level of existence. There can be no real lack or scarcity; there is nothing we have to try to achieve or attract; we contain the potential for everything within us.

Manifestation through creative visualization is the process of realizing and making visible on the physical plane our divine potential.

Discovering Our Higher Purpose

A basic need of all human beings is to make a positive contribution to the world and to our fellow beings, as well as to improve and enjoy our personal lives. We all have a great deal to offer the world and to each other, each in our own special and unique way. To a great degree, our own personal sense of well being is a function of how much we are expressing this.

We each have a significant contribution to make in this lifetime. It may involve many things, or it may be something very simple. I call this contribution our higher purpose. It always involves being yourself totally, completely, and naturally, and doing something or many things that you genuinely love to do, and that come easily to you.

We all know in our hearts what our higher purpose is, but we often do not consciously acknowledge it, even to ourselves. In fact, most people seem to go to great lengths to hide it from themselves and from the world. They fear and seek to avoid the power, responsibility, and light that comes with acknowledging and expressing their true purpose in life.

As you use creative visualization, you will find that you become more and more attuned to and aware of your higher purpose. Notice the elements that tend to recur in your dreams, goals, and fantasies, the particular qualities that are there in the things you find yourself doing and creating. These are important clues to the underlying meaning and purpose of your life.

You will find in using creative visualization that your ability to manifest will work to the degree that you are in alignment with your higher purpose. If you try to manifest something and it doesn't seem to work, it may not be appropriate to the underlying pattern and meaning of your life. Be patient and keep tuning into your inner guidance. In retrospect you will see that everything is unfolding perfectly.

This is a time of great transformation on our planet. We all have a part to play, just by being willing to be our true, magnificent selves.

Your Life is Your Work of Art

I like to think of myself as an artist, and my life is my greatest work of art. Every moment is a moment of creation, and each moment of creation contains infinite possibilities. I can do things the way I've always done them, or I can look at all the different alternatives, and try something new and different and potentially more rewarding. Every moment presents a new opportunity and a new decision.

What a wonderful game we are all playing, and what a magnificent art form. . . .

Recommended Reading and Study

Books

Tantra for the West—A Guide to Personal Freedom by Marcus Allen. Whatever Publishing 1981. An excellent companion volume to *Creative Visualization*. Tantra is far more than just the yoga of sex—it is the yoga of *every moment*. The principle of tantra is applied to the most important areas of our lives: relationships, sex, being alone, work, money, creativity, food and drink, meditation and yoga, aging and healing, politics, enlightenment, and freedom.

Reunion: Tools for Transformation by Mark Allen and Shakti Gawain. Whatever Publishing 1978. This book contains many of the most simple, clear, and effective teachings and practices which the authors have encountered. Part I: Opening; Part II: Understanding; Part III: Tools for Transformation; Part IV: Now We're Free!

The Nature of Personal Reality (A Seth Book) by Jane Roberts. Prentice Hall 1974. An excellent explanation of how we are each totally responsible for creating our own reality. Very highly recommended.

The Silva Mind Control Method by Jose Silva and Philip Miele. Simon and Schuster 1977. Contains explanations and practices in creative visualization by one of the modern pioneers in the field.

Pray and Grow Rich by Catherine Ponder. Parker Publishing Co. 1968. Also many other books by Catherine

Ponder, including *The Prospering Power of Love, The Dynamic Laws of Prosperity, The Dynamic Laws of Healing*. These books have sensationalistic covers and a Christian orientation which may not appeal to some, but I have found them to contain deep understanding and a wonderful variety of techniques and affirmations.

The Art of Spiritual Healing by Joel Goldsmith. Harper and Row 1957. Also many others by the same author, such as: *The Art of Meditation, The Infinite Way, Practicing the Presence.* Written by a great healer, these books are channeled from a place of deep understanding. I have found them profoundly helpful and inspiring.

An Idea Whose Time Has Come (The Hunger Project Source Book) by Werner Erhard 1977. Explains how we can each effectively take responsibility for ending hunger on earth within the next twenty years. A very powerful example of how changing our own belief system can transform the entire planet as well as our own lives. Very highly recommended to all. Write to: The Hunger Project, P.O. Box 789, San Francisco, Ca. 94101. Send $2.00 per book ordered.

The Art of True Healing by Israel Regardie. Samuel Weiser. A small book containing a system of creative visualization derived from the teachings of the Kabbala. The meditation on opening the energy centers is derived from the middle pillar meditation described in this book.

Kinship With All Life by J. Allen Boone. Harper and Row 1976. A unique and beautiful book. Although primarily concerned with human relationships with animals, it contains deep wisdom and insight about the use of visualization and affirmation in all relationships.

The Findhorn Garden by the Findhorn Community. Harper and Row 1975. One of the most beautiful and inspiring books I've ever read; it's about how we can communicate and cooperate with all forms of life and all of nature.

Handbook to Higher Consciousness by Ken Keyes, Jr. Living Love Publishing 1975. A very clear explanation of how our own "programming" creates our experience of reality. This book is especially helpful in learning to flow more easily through life.

Mystic Path to Cosmic Power by Vernon Howard. Prentice-Hall 1967. Channeled wisdom from a high, clear perspective.

Rebirthing in the New Age by Leonard Orr and Sondra Ray. Celestial Arts 1977. An explanation of how our basic beliefs are often adopted at the moment of birth.

I Deserve Love by Sondra Ray. Les Femmes 1976. Contains many good affirmations dealing with our attitudes about love and sex.

Manifestation by David Spangler. The Findhorn Foundation. This tiny booklet contains advanced wisdom on the art of creative visualization. Write to: The Findhorn Foundation, The Park, Forres, Moray, Scotland.

Tapes

Creative Visualization, a 60-minute cassette by Shakti Gawain designed to accompany this book. Shakti guides you on a meditation journey involving deep relaxation, visualizing a goal, opening energy centers, affirmations, and more. Listening repeatedly has a deep effect upon your consciousness, which will manifest as wonderful change in your daily life.

Stress Reduction and Creative Meditations, a 40-minute cassette by Marcus Allen. Side One is a twenty-minute guided deep relaxation process; Side Two has guided meditations for producing health, abundance, and fulfillment. With soothing background music by Jon Bernoff.

14 Days to a Wellness Lifestyle, a 90-minute cassette by Dr. Donald Ardell. Backed by beautiful classical music, Dr. Ardell guides listeners through his 14-day program which assists them in establishing lifelong patterns of high-level wellness and maximum performance.

Music

Breathe. An instrumental musical journey performed by Jon Bernoff and Marcus Allen. Enjoyable, calming music that creates a beautiful soundscape for meditative listening, and a peaceful home or office environment. LP or cassette.

Petals. Floating, peaceful, melodic instrumental music. Creates a beautiful soundscape, whether you're deeply listening or using it as a background/environmental piece. LP or cassette.

All of the above tapes and records (and more) are available from Whatever Publishing, P.O. Box 137, Mill Valley, CA 94941. Write or phone for a free catalog. Phone: (415) 388-2100. Phone toll free for orders: (800) 227-3900; in California: (800) 632-2122.

Other

I would like to acknowledge the Unity Church, and Church of Religious Science as the source of some of my material.

ABOUT THE AUTHOR

SHAKTI GAWAIN has a gift for blending the rational approach of the Western mind with the deep, intuitive wisdom of the East. She studied psychology and dance at Reed College and the University of California. After graduation she traveled for two years in Europe and Asia, studying Eastern philosophy, meditation, and yoga.

When she returned to America, she continued to delve deeply into her own personal growth, reading extensively and studying with many well-known teachers in the human potential movement. Her continuing exploration of philosophy and psychology has culminated in the writing of her bestselling book, *Creative Visualization*.

Shakti Gawain now lives in Mill Valley, California, where she leads workshops and classes on creative visualization and related subjects.

BANTAM NEW AGE BOOKS

Bantam New Age Books are for all those interested in reflecting on life today and life as it may be in the future. This important new imprint features stimulating works in fields from biology and psychology to philosophy and the new physics.

☐	25388	**DON'T SHOOT THE DOG** Karen Pryor	$3.95
☐	25344	**SUPERMIND: THE ULTIMATE ENERGY** Barbara B. Brown	$4.95
☐	24147	**CREATIVE VISUALIZATION** Shatki Gawain	$3.95
☐	24903	**NEW RULES: SEARCHING FOR SELF-FULFILLMENT IN A WORLD TURNED UPSIDE DOWN** Daniel Yankelovich	$4.50
☐	25223	**STRESS AND THE ART OF BIOFEEDBACK** Barbara Brown	$4.95
☐	24682	**THE FIRST THREE MINUTES** Steven Weinberg	$3.95
☐	20005	**MAGICAL CHILD** Joseph Chilton Pearce	$3.95
☐	25748	**ZEN/MOTORCYCLE MAINTENANCE** Robert Pirsig	$4.95
☐	20693	**THE WAY OF THE SHAMAN** Michael Hamer	$3.95
☐	25437	**TO HAVE OR TO BE** Fromm	$4.50
☐	24562	**LIVES OF A CELL** Lewis Thomas	$3.95
☐	14912	**KISS SLEEPING BEAUTY GOODBYE** K. Kolbenschlag	$3.95

Prices and availability subject to change without notice.

Buy them at your local bookstore or use this handy coupon:

Bantam Books. Inc., Dept NA, 414 East Golf Road, Des Plaines, Ill. 60016

Please send me the books I have checked above. I am enclosing $_____
(please add $1.50 to cover postage and handling). Send check or money order
—no cash or C.O.D.'s please.

Mr/Mrs/Miss _____

Address _____

City _____ State/Zip _____

NA—1/86

Please allow four to six weeks for delivery. This offer expires 7/86.

BANTAM
SHOP·AT·HOME
C·A·T·A·L·O·G

Special Offer
Buy a Bantam Book
for only 50¢.

Now you can have an up-to-date listing of Bantam's hundreds of titles plus take advantage of our unique and exciting bonus book offer. A special offer which gives you the opportunity to purchase a Bantam book for only 50¢. Here's how!

By ordering any five books at the regular price per order, you can also choose any other single book listed (up to a $4.95 value) for just 50¢. Some restrictions do apply, but for further details why not send for Bantam's listing of titles today!

Just send us your name and address and we will send you a catalog!